For Raphael

THE LIFE AND MUSIC OF
NICK CAVE
AN ILLUSTRATED BIOGRAPHY

written by **Maximilian Dax**

translated by **Ian Minock**

designed by **Johannes Beck**

Contents

Chapter 1 . . . . **At Home**   13

Chapter 2 . . . . **London**   31

Chapter 3 . . . . **Junk**   49

Chapter 4 . . . . **Berlin**   65

Chapter 5 . . . . **Blues**   83

Chapter 6 . . . . **Ghosts** 105

Chapter 7 . . . . **Gringo** 123

Chapter 8 . . . . **Amen** 147

The visuals 171

The photographers 172

Discography 173

The authors 174

The publisher 175

Preface

…No, it is impossible; it is impossible to convey the life-sensation of any given epoch of one's existence, – that which makes its truth, its meaning – its subtle and penetrating essence. It is impossible. We live, as we dream – alone. …

Joseph Conrad, 'Heart of Darkness'

Life is full of special moments that pass in a blink of an eye. So, what can we really say about this endless succession of fleeting episodes we call life? I personally see biographies and photos for that matter in the same way I look upon death. A biography is an attempt at keeping hold of something that can never be preserved. In December 1998, Robert Klanten, head of Die Gestalten Verlag, asked me whether I could imagine taking on an illustrated biography of the life of Nick Cave. At first, I didn't know what to say. It was only when my good friend Max Dax offered to work with me that I was able to tell Robert to give the book the go-ahead. Max and I were less interested in Nick Cave the rock-star and didn't think that simply producing another work on the mystery of the man or perpetuating naive rock'n'roll myths would do the singer justice. We have therefore elected to publish our book as an attractive alternative to the usual ridiculous and out-dated notions that already abound. Delving deep into the Nick Cave phenomenon meant that we had to plough our way through container loads of playlists, liner notes, interviews, critiques, background information, and gossip – as well as scrutinising several tons of photo material.

In our selection of photos and informative stories about the great singer, we have tried not to lose track of the various periods and paradigms in the Nick Cave story. The story of his life and the challenges and sources of inspiration that mattered turned Nick into a symbol of a whole generation, as future dissertations will confirm. Working on this book frequently gave rise to discussions that led us to look at our own pasts. We somehow embarked on a journey to learn more about the workings of biographies, to ascertain, finally, that we were, in fact, recording history. In a time when blatant and meaningless hedonism has taken the place of religion and culture is defined by high-handedness, it is essential that we take note of people who have remained true to themselves and kept their stance. Nick Cave is undeniably a person of that ilk. Perhaps we have succeeded in our attempts at creating a heartening atmosphere of light, colour, and words, and we hope it offers an authentic taste of the gripping events of another time and place. This book would never had come about had our publisher, Robert Klanten, not given us an absolutely free hand in the design concept and content. Thank you.

Johannes Beck
September 1999

At Home

Some fools would be all the better, not only for having their hair pulled, but for a good drubbing.

Feodor M. Dostojevski, 'Crime and Punishment'

By the time Nicholas Edward Cave, age 12, was expelled from Wangaratta High School in Victoria in 1970, the Commonwealth of Australia was busy sending some of its finest young men to help fight the American war in Vietnam. Although Nicholas Edward's conduct was anything but exemplary at the best of times, the authorities decided that they had had enough of his irreverent attitude when he and one of his classmates were caught red-handed trying to remove the underwear of a girl four years their senior in a hormone-induced exploit. That wasn't all. His persistent brawling and disruptive influence didn't contribute much to enhance his image, either. Nicholas Edward's father, Colin, an English teacher at the school, and his mother, Dawn, one of the school librarians, were both horrified at their son's involvement in this 'attempted rape' and sent him off to boarding school in Melbourne 130 miles away. However, any hopes they might have had that their wayward offspring would be brought to his senses by Caulfield Grammar School's stringent rule of command were soon dashed. The self-control the regime at Caulfield expected from students was something Nick Cave refused to ascribe to. He was still getting into scraps, while his flaunting of the school rules soon made him stand out, so his peers started to regard him as something of a provocateur. Luckily, there were several other students in the same year as Nick who also had an obvious disregard for authority and, in next to no time, they had formed their own little circle. These students soon came to realise that they all shared a common interest in the latest music from England, and now that the big international record companies had made up their minds to conquer the Australian market, Nick and his school friends were able to get their hands on new records not long after their release in the UK. David Bowie, Brian Eno and Roxy Music were much more fascinating to Nick's circle than the whole of the domestic music scene put together. The material Australian bands were playing in the late seventies was a simple rehash of chart hits, but glam rock, and later punk and new wave, were at once raucous and liberating. As only specialist record store stocked these imports, they were relatively expensive, but this made them even more desirable, and Nick's circle of public schoolboys could hardly wait to invest their pocket-money in the most recent arrivals. Before long, they came to develop a taste for harder music, especially the wild and untamed rock of Iggy Pop and The Sensational Alex Harvey Band, whose sound was not too difficult to imitate. In 1974, just for the hell of it, Nick and five of his best friends thought it might be fun to form a band themselves. This decision would give rise to The Boys Next Door three years later, and The Birthday Party, a further two years down the line. Not long after the dogma of virtuosity had been shaken to the core by the advent of punk, the seemingly never-ending flow of new and exciting records from rock's traditional homelands had finally moved Nick Cave and the members of the school band, Mick Harvey and John Cochivera on guitar, Phill Calvert on drums, saxophonist Chris Coyne, and Brett Purcell on bass, to take matters into their own hands.

Seventeen years old in 1974, Nicholas Edward Cave was born on 22 September 1957. Nick had two older brothers, Tim and Peter, as well as a younger sister, Julie, and as a young man had long dreamt of becoming a celebrated artist who would travel the world and meet interesting people. At Caulfield, his long hair and eye-catching socks complemented his school uniform in an overtly impudent kind of way, but the main features that set Nick Cave apart from his peers were his flamboyant nature and diffuse inquisitiveness about the experiences a man could only make to the full by running the risk of receiving permanent scars. He was cocky without being insensitive, knew how to use humour to get ahead, and sensed that his intuition would somehow reveal to him the path he should follow. It was a form of magnetism that drove him to seek out danger, as if surviving difficult situations gave him new insights, not just into the intricacies of life itself, but into his own psychic make-up as well. There were times when he would play the hyperactive clown, pushing his schoolmates into swimming pools, but woe betide anybody who dared to give him the same rough treatment. While Victoria baked in the heat of the sun, Nick, Mick and Phill were getting bored with their fellow schoolmates' conviction that having fun meant lounging about on beaches all afternoon, doing their homework, and going to

extra-curricular PE. Being the centre of attention in a band offered Nick's circle no number of welcome opportunities to rebel against the bourgeois values around them. And it didn't matter that they couldn't actually play their instruments well enough to pen anything of great artistic value. Instead, the lads let off steam through their barefaced theatrical gestures. Their upfront attitudes and the benefit of their young years allowed them to face off outsiders who scoffed at the band's rebellious pathos and the unfocused song-writing ambitions of its lead singer. This cad-like arrogance was the band's tactic of displaying a desire to be different from those who were firmly stuck in the school-system rut.

As performers, the members of the band hit the stage with the uncorrupted courage of the young and raised the roof, strutting their stuff for audiences who were witness to all this juvenile madness. The band's repertoire was exclusively comprised of other people's material, and performances were usually at barbecues or in the school hall. In particular, the friends enjoyed playing at Shelford Girls' Grammar School next door. Even though Caulfield caused Nick Cave more than a few headaches, he pursued his interests with dedication. He took advantage of the numerous courses offered at the school, took piano lessons, and went to art classes, fascinated by books on its history and the great painters. His interest in religious studies was nearly as great as his passion for literature. Nick would write poetry in the privacy of his own home, which his parents had left in the meantime to move to Melbourne. There is a photo of Nick's class in their final year at Caulfield Grammar that shows him with his trousers down, his face well hidden behind a long mane of hair. Life with Nick was never dull. He was prepared to stand up to his teachers and wasn't afraid to defy convention. Alcohol and cigarettes were cheap, and drugs, reputed to broaden the mind, were a new experience he and his friends could always check out. The Cave circle finished school in 1976, passing their exams with distinction. Those who had thought of the band as no more than a typical high school pastime weren't expecting it to hold together, now that school was out for good, and were quite surprised when, in fact, it did. There were changes to the line-up, however. There was no longer room for Chris and his giant saxophone. Tracy Pew, a cute, wild type of kid, obsessed by literature, was a close friend of Nick's and replaced Brett Purcell on bass. Purcell's concept of what made a good band wouldn't have fitted in with the anarchic nature of the others, anyway. Suddenly, John Cochivera's time was up when his parents insisted on sending him off to live with relatives in America. He and Nick had taken their first tab of LSD together after which he had spent days dazed and confused. Mick Harvey was a vicar's son with a quiet, wistful nature that established him as the backbone of the band. However, he didn't believe that being in a group was simply a question of playing other people's material, so he set off on his own for a while, only to come back into the fold at an open-air concert at Mount Waverly in Victoria. Life just wasn't the same without his music.

In 1976 the boys from Down Under began to sense that being in a rock band was going to have a profound effect on defining their identities. They lopped off their long hair and started sporting 1950s-style crew cuts, becoming all the more dashing in the process, while their jeans and T-shirts gave way to second-hand suits, shirts, and ties from the Salvation Army's 'Golden Ops' stores, gestures that enabled the former public schoolboys to put their pasts behind them once and for all. It also offered them the perfect opportunity to give the band a name. Nick had already made a number of suggestions, 'Vulture Culture' among them, but the name they all finally settled on was 'The Boys Next Door'. Their first gig was in Mick Harvey's father's church hall in August 1977, and although Mick's dad didn't quite approve of his son's being in a band, he had no other option than to put up or shut up. The gig ended in a brawl provoked by a horde of skinheads who saw the concert as the ideal setting to give what they saw as a bunch of well-to-do's something to remember them by.

Nick Cave enrolled at Caulfield Technical College in 1976. A Victorian school of art, its heritage was reflected in its traditionally structured curriculum that covered landscapes, portraits and nude painting, but little else. He was greeted with open arms thanks to his distinct artistic talent but took no great interest in the recognition the staid college was prepared to bestow on him. The eighteen months Nick spent there were more an incitement to cross boundaries just to see how far he could go, his confrontation a convenient tool for provoking his betters. Nick never tired of shocking his art teacher with his tendency to devote a great deal of his time portraying genitalia, and he frequently turned up for class worse the wear for drink. Cave's flirt with the conservative college didn't last long, as he didn't see the point in wasting his time arguing with professors who couldn't comprehend his taste for pornography or his passion for Romanesque and Gothic religious icons. Above all, the realisation that he could exasperate people without too much effort with his obsessions, real or otherwise, marked Nick Cave for life. He came to know a few up-and-coming artists at Caulfield Technical College including his girlfriend, Anita Lane. Like himself, this crowd was not interested in perfecting the academic side to their artistic talents, instead aspiring to a bohemian lifestyle. The way people reacted to the rebellious lead singer of The Boys Next Door during that time was also to change Nick Cave's life forever. Although he had attended the

college with relentless regularity, it ceased to be the focal point of his daily disputes with the irrational at the beginning of autumn 1977. He now started to see that being on stage was the perfect platform for demonstrating to the world just how provocative he could be. His reward for his return to music was a grateful and faithful audience which, at that time, was mainly comprised of a broader circle of friends and acquaintances. The band was proof of what it was like to live free from the middle-class conventions and regulations that were fiercely upheld in Melbourne, just like everywhere else in the Western world. Audiences of between 20 and 100 paying guests faithfully turned up time and time again to see the boys perform in pubs, crowds shrinking after a poor gig but growing after a good one. The Boys Next Door were regarded as a good drinking band, and with their in-your-face attitudes, they created a fan base that adored their scandalous performances and their shifty style.

By 1978, the music of the Sex Pistols and the Pop Group had reached Australian shores and thoroughly appealed to the musicians' sense of individuality. The Boys Next Door weren't just about copying the music style The Stooges had created, which had found a contemporary voice in the aggressive punk rock of the Sex Pistols. More important to The Boys Next Door was finding enough courage to believe in their own musical expression, thus allowing them to perform it in public with a sense of pride. Australian music magazines tended to deride the musical revolution that in England had taken the country by storm, its effects felt at every level of society. Australian editors considered fans as nothing more than a small circle of weird characters and simply refused to cater for their tastes. Music journalists regarded punk as an insignificant and decadent trend and therefore failed to notice that this music was already inspiring a multitude of Australian musicians who played in bands that had yet to find a voice. Many had already assumed a rebellious attitude but believed they were solitary fighters, alone in the vastness of Australia. Unobserved by the music press, a new musical culture had taken root in Australia that wasn't entrenched in the country-pop scene. For the first time, musicians were willing to go further than simply imitating chart-storming rock idols from America.

The mainstream music press in ultra-conservative Australia was blind to these new developments. Of course, there were a few punk fanzines with tiny readerships that did take heed of fans' views or offered them a platform to exchange information and ideas, but they remained obscure, the one exception, an underground rag called Rock Australia Magazine, printed and published in Sydney. Rock Australia was an exotic alternative, a welcome voice for fans of independent groups such as

The Saints, The Four Gods, The Go-Betweens and Super K from Brisbane, The Reels from Dubbo, The Brutish X from Sydney, or The Young Charlatans and The Boys Next Door from Melbourne, all of whom appreciated its superior quality to the xeroxed fanzines they were familiar with. Rowland S. Howard, later to become an influential member of The Boys Next Door and The Birthday Party, contributed to Rock Australia Magazine as well as a number of short-lived minor punk fanzines. Howard, who played guitar and sang in the Young Charlatans, wrote in Pulp-Fanzine in 1976 that The Boys Next Door were 'the best Rock'n'Roll band in Melbourne'. The supposedly best Rock'n'-Roll band in Melbourne was just starting to make a name for itself as the first generation of independently minded new wave bands were coming to understand that they, too, had a justified right to express their music as they saw fit. Nothing would ever be the same again. Luckily, Nick Cave and his band just happened to be at the hub of this new and exciting Australian scene and were taking Melbourne's stages by storm.

In the 1970s, Melbourne, a city with a vast suburban sprawl, was still trapped in a Victorian time warp. The first generation of young people who had neither experienced the War or the economic boom of the 50s and 60s no longer believed in the same old values as their elders. People had been taking to the streets to demonstrate against the war in Vietnam and protesters were unhappy at the role Australia had played in sending small contingents of soldiers into combat there. Everyday life seemed increasingly unsufferable. New wave in its Australian incarnation was mainly a private affair and was welcomed by many as an excuse for dressing up in the latest fashions. Others saw it as a vehicle for voicing their frustrations at the established traditions of a huge country which, for far too long, had complacently basked in the sun. New music in Australia embraced a much broader plethora of styles than it had back in England and was more what would be described as 'independent' music today. Nor did it have any real political content, its message watered down on its long journey from Europe. The Australian scene hadn't yet developed its own established structures, unlike in England where the beat generation had heralded a musical revolution many years before. And concepts that raised questions on where society was going such as Malcolm McClaren's Sex Pistols and Vivienne Westwood, whose Warholesque designs reflected a 'Fuck Everybody' philosophy, were regarded by people Down Under as exotic and the underlying message didn't quite have the same ring there as it did in the UK. Still, people were starting to feel that things were genuinely changing. The Boys Next Door were an integral part of this unfocused counter-movement, but as Rowland S. Howard had correctly assessed, were not much more than an ordinary pop band. Not that this actually mattered because, when it came

down to basics, the band's attitude, illustrated in their chaotic, drunken, wild performances was, by all accounts, punk.

The musicians had plenty to get on with during this turbulent phase in their lives. Their gigs were fun and exuberant, fuelled by excessive amounts of alcohol and whatever else was the toast of the day, and they survived the processes they had set in motion with their strong sense of humour intact. After all, they were a circle of privileged former public school boys who had come to realise that poking a finger at society was fun. Along the lines that whoever usually gets everything right, rarely does anything wrong, The Boys Next Door made a conscious endeavour not only to satisfy their fans but, during those first few months, were also willing to run the risk of alienating them. They came across as a surreptitious circle of conspicuously dressed trouble-makers, an attitude that didn't stop The Boys Next Door from signing up with Suicide Records. Suicide was the first Australian label to sign up new Australian punk and new wave bands in addition to distributing music from overseas. The parent company, Mushroom, was looking to profit from the imminent boom it expected to hit the domestic scene and did its utmost to systematically secure copyrights. However, there was no set of guidelines that allowed for any in-depth cooperation between the label and its signings. A live sampler entitled 'Lethal Weapons' that featured three of The Boys Next Door songs alongside tracks by young bands such as the Teenage Radio Stars, JAB, The Negatives and the Survivors was subsequently released as a one-off unlucky compromise. Barry Earl, Suicide's manager, had insisted on easily accessible songs such as 'These Boots Are Made For Walking', a Boys Next Door cover of the Lee Hazlewood/Nancy Sinatra classic, and their own composition, 'Masturbation Generation', which people would recognise from their concerts. The only new material was the Mick Harvey track 'Boy Hero'.

The songs themselves were not the problem, as bootlegged cuts of concerts the boys played around that time adequately document. The difficulty lay more in the fact that Suicide insisted on cleaning up the recordings so that radio stations could broadcast them. This took away much of the songs' authenticity and edge, something the band had taken great care to foster at their concerts. For The Boys Next Door this accident was an unpleasant reminder that their naivety was still more pronounced than their powers of persuasion, a warning shot that made them prick up their ears. There was one consolation, however: radio stations declined to play the songs. Up until then, Nick Cave hadn't put great value on perspicacity. The relationship that had developed between him and Rowland S. Howard inspired Nick to tackle his lyrics more critically and to take a more analytical approach that went a lot further than just making songs rhyme. Anita Lane openly voiced her opinions on Nick's work and thought the lines *'People down in the city square are losing their mind and they are losing their hair, yeah, yeah, yeah'* were ridiculous, and told him so. Nick had penned a few ambitious songs but had wallowed in pathos in others, using it as a smokescreen to hide behind. But it didn't take him long to realise that trying to keep out of the line of fire was a strategy bound to fail. The band started to see life as an adventure and tried to put some distance between themselves and the difficulties they were facing both within the band and in the world outside. Along with some of the groups featured on the 'Lethal Weapons' sampler, The Boys Next Door had just returned from a tour organised by Suicide and were now back in Melbourne playing hell-raising gigs at venues all over town. They were beginning to play more and more of their own material and even if their lyrics weren't exactly profound or full of cryptic meaning, they were unquestionably starting to take shape. Concert highlights included a cover version of The Velvet Underground's 'Caroline Says' and an adaptation of The Ramones hit 'Blitzkrieg Bop'.

In 1978, The Boys Next Door were one of Melbourne's biggest attractions. Their concerts were wild and unpredictable, no two were ever the same, and their inherent anarchism made people sit up and take notice. Fans loved songs like 'Masturbation Generation'. Clubbers, on the other hand, were a bit unsure of how to take them and the police were totally up in arms. Whenever security tried to get the band to calm down a notch or two, Nick Cave and Mick Harvey would retort with Nazi salutes and cries of 'Sieg Heil!', stopping the proceedings without a care for their own safety or that of their fans in the front rows. There are no videos of the concerts of these days, but bootlegs and memories testify to the band's extraordinary committment to an extreme form of haughty hedonism. Nick's slender frame and his hyper-energy drew people's attention at concerts. He would writhe around on the floor, jump off the stage into the pit, and expertly deploy pathos in his performance to heighten the impact of his personal messages to the world. Mick Harvey's on-stage persona was more reserved. He preferred observing goings-on from afar and was the epitome of calm amidst this over-the-top chaos. Mick's expertise on guitar always had the desired effect, accompanied by Phill Calvert and the usually pissed Tracy Pew, the final pieces in the puzzle that fused the group into a rock-solid entity.

The band gave off an aura of glamour: The Boys Next Door were rebellious but loveable, young – and anything but innocent. They were rough, sexy and dangerous, even if much of it was a put-on. The musicians were able to incorporate the experiences they made on-stage into their daily routines, including

their penchant for being loud, the alcohol and the free rein they were given. Most of all, the band gave Nick all the encouragement and support he needed for his exaggerated stage performances by forming an appropriate backdrop for the diffuse anti-establishment attitudes of their audiences. The band's vigorous live performances showed just how hard-baked the four of them were. Accidents in stolen cars, arrests for masturbating in public as well as for drunken binges that ended in destroying telephone boxes and wash-hand basins in pub toilets, bear witness to just how unruly these young men really were.

Competition among bands from the class of 1978 had virtually sprung up overnight. Whether in Sydney, Melbourne or Brisbane, the Australian music scene was gathering momentum, and this fascination with underground music suddenly inspired bands to do just as well as their English heroes. At the same time, nobody had any real idea of how to keep the ball rolling, once the initial euphoria had ebbed. Touring bands like The Talking Heads, Blondie, The TV Personalities, The Ramones, The Cramps and Suicide were the only way Australians could witness first-hand what had been happening abroad. The Boys Next Door tried hard in those difficult months to smooth over the impression they had left behind after the release of 'Lethal Weapon' by being more aggressive in their stage performances. Under pressure and realising that nothing seemed to stand still for any amount of time, they became more creative, although, at that moment in their lives, it looked like diffuse machinations were driving them towards individual careers. Nonetheless, the band members still found time to enjoy themselves in the midst of decline and increasingly hardening fronts, and alcohol and drugs were welcome tools in their shameless celebration of who and what they were. The band responded with bafflement to fans' reactions to their various attempts at defining their own brand of music. The music press, for its part, was totally outpaced by their continual style changes and new song compilations, adding insult to injury by making it extremely difficult for fans to comprehend The Boys Next Door's regular transformations.

A lucky coincidence did much to promote the band's sense of creative awareness when, in the summer of 1978, they were offered a regular engagement at The Crystal Ballroom, an unorthodox location in Melbourne's St Kilda red-light district near the edge of town. The Crystal Ballroom hosted a whole lot of events such as public readings, film shoots, and rock concerts, with different bands playing particular slots. The Boys Next Door were to play in St Kilda in the Saturday afternoon opening that had arisen. The Crystal Ballroom was, of course, an illusion, a utopia, a new wave dream of a better world. The fact that there were so many young people with so many varied interests

2 CUTE CUNTS

2 CUTE CUNTS

concentrated in one place led to an exchange of views and experiments that often led them down tortuous paths. New bands were founded and split up all the time. Nevertheless, the Crystal Ballroom was the perfect setting for much mutual learning among the phalanx of musicians who frequented it.

St Kilda itself was a dilapidated former entertainment district and housed much of Melbourne's beach and nightlife. After dark, it was dominated by prostitution, poverty, alcoholism, hard drugs and the tales elderly immigrant Jews from Nazi Germany, who had never returned home, told about life there. During the day St Kilda was a haven for tourists who loved its beaches. It was a place where young, vigorous cliques of egocentric bohemians lived in an illusion of being far removed from the bourgeois values and rules of a forgotten world. St Kilda's narrow little streets were teeming with cinemas, second-hand shops and snack-bars. For The Boys Next Door it was paradise on earth. And it was here that they made the acquaintance of a new and very close friend: heroin.

Nick Cave enjoyed the cosmopolitan feeling of St Kilda, and the drugs he was taking there gave him a new awareness. He felt quite at home in the underworld of the district where crime was rife and drugs were sold openly in the streets. Its generic decadence became a part of normal everyday life. In the same way as generations of cinema goers before them had been captivated by the gangster myths of smoky jazz clubs and the seedy bars pimps and their girls hung out in, the young generation in St Kilda saw in the criminal at large an outlaw figure worthy of their respect. St Kilda gave people a chance to take a much more romantic approach to the grim reality of the neighbourhood. Anita Lane, as an artist and part of The Boys Next Door clique, used to participate in literary and philosophical debates at the Crystal Ballroom and remembers that there were quite a few Italo-Australian Mafiosi in the area. Once, in a novel attempt at intimidation, one of them even bit her. The experiences Nick and Anita and the rest of the circle made in St Kilda's twilight world were somehow instilling in them a new-found confidence which brought them closer together. They began to see the band's positive attributes in a new light, reflected it in their music and their dress, and developed a new, more serious attitude towards their purpose. In short, they polished up their act. The price they had to pay, however, was that some of their fans began to see their stage performances as increasingly arrogant and snobbish. There wasn't really a lot the musicians could do, except drive on and still find time for some enjoyment in intoxication during these challenging times.

1978 saw much of the band's activities become Rock'n'Roll routine. Rowland S. Howard was more involved with the band by this stage, and his proficiency on the guitar as well as his song-writing talents were becoming indispensable. United, the group set off on a tour of the East Coast, sharing the billing with some of the bands they admired such as The Go-Betweens and an early line-up of Crime and the City Solution, whose lead singer, Simon Bonny, and his dramatic stage shows had left a lasting impression on Nick Cave. The general feeling of having lost their way which had become quite pronounced a few months prior to Howard's joining the band full-time gradually began to dissipate in 1978. Things were starting to look up.

The Boys Next Door's tour was followed by two studio sessions, the first without Howard, and the second six months later which was defined by his outstanding talents. The musicians recorded the material for the band's first and last regular album, 'Door, Door', which was released in 1979. Although they were naturally driven by the hope that the record would sell well, market logic wasn't the only reason behind the album. Nick Cave had learned so much from his exchanges with Simon Bonny and, more importantly, Rowland. S. Howard. The realisation that home-grown Australian talent could successfully find new ways of expressing itself on its own back doorstep was playing an ever-increasing role in how Nick was quantifying his own status.

For Tracy Pew, being drunk had become a normal state of affairs. Rowland, Phill and Nick saw heroin, whenever available, as a good substitute for alcohol and were using it more and more. And it didn't give you a hangover. However, not even drugs and the prospects of having the chance to live any life-style they pleased could paper over the cracks that were now appearing within the band. Mick and Rowland both played guitar and were embroiled in a battle of wits, Mick eventually relegated to the synth, a strangely displaced instrument in The Boys Next Door. Nick and Rowland weren't very good at hiding their respective contention for control, either, and the tension was becoming untenable. Amidst all this turbulence, Colin Cave, Nick's father was killed in a tragic car accident on 11 October 1978, a few days after his son's 21st birthday. This tragedy triggered a deep depression. Nick had lost a loved one at a time when he had been trying to make life difficult for his father. This sudden loss left behind a feeling of enduring power-lessness. If Keith Glass hadn't turned up on the scene at the end of 1978, the potential split The Boys Next Door were facing may have seen Nick Cave's musical career evaporate in the hot sand of the Australian desert before it had really taken off.

Keith Glass owned the Missing Link record store in Melbourne, the top address for imported records from London and New York, where Phill Calvert worked behind the counter.

When, in 1979, Glass suggested taking on The Boys Next Door as their manager, it seemed to all concerned like the obvious step to take. Glass's enthusiasm also implied an intrinsic good sense for business, and he was genuinely convinced that Nick Cave and the rest of the band should try their luck in London, the centre of the pop world. Flights to England didn't come cheap, and any money the band had earned in 1978 and 1979 from their gigs had been squandered on drugs and alcohol. It was down to Glass's influence that the musicians started to put aside a large chunk of the money they were earning to pay for their flight tickets to Europe. Now that they had something to work towards, The Boys Next Door felt inspired to repay the trust shown them and started to produce material of a new aggressive quality. They mused with assuming pseudonyms for a short time: Nick thought 'Nicky Danger' might suit him, Rowland had opted for 'Johnny America', Phill for 'Phill Thump', and Tracy would only answer to 'Buddy Love'. This was all drunken banter and served to fuse the band together in a street-gang kind of way and was a good line of attack to avoid any black eyes. That was the frame of mind The Boys Next Door were in when 'Door, Door' was released.

In retrospect, this ten-track album of innocuous pop songs, released on the Mushroom label in 1979 and again on compact disc by Mute in 1993, is an astounding document of just how much a record company can compromise a band's artistic identity. The first six tracks on 'Door, Door', recorded in 1978 during the first studio session and without Rowland, hint at what the band was all about but practically smother the charm of the songs due to an unfortunately ignorant production. The band's lack of studio experience is conspicuous and the instruments were recorded individually instead of as a live ensemble – and it shows, the studio versions therefore lacking the energy and intensity of the band's concerts. Cave's voice is melo-dramatic, the arrangements predictable, and the style seems to emulate the groups The Boys Next Door looked up to when they were just starting out. The rest of the tracks on the album show more ambition, but even here it is patent that Rowland's desire to write pop songs didn't really fit in with the anti-estab-lishment attitude the band upheld. Instead of documenting what The Boys Next Door stood for, these songs, especially those written by Nick and Rowland, testify to a strange desire to be left alone.

'Shivers', the fruit of a poorly concealed rivalry, was the single taken from the album and starts with the lyrics *'I've been contemplating suicide / But it really doesn't suit my style'*. The live version of the song, the band usually wide-eyed on speed in a performance that was completely over the top, was re-ceived enthusiastically by audiences, but appears listless when taken out of context. The band was aghast when 'Door, Door' was acclaimed by critics and sold 4,000 copies within a short period. They were glad that their departure for London would soon be upon them. Encouraged by the trust Glass had shown them and after a series of sessions in Melbourne's Richmond Recorder Studios, The Boys Next Door started writing new, more upbeat material that now reverberated with their energy and determination. The band was working with the same sound engineer, Tony Cohen, who had worked with them on the second half of 'Door, Door', the only person after Keith Glass to recognise what was going on in Cave's and Rowland's creative minds. The band soon also came to appreciate the technical potential offered by the studio which, in itself, was an additional musical instrument that could come in useful for musical experiments. Rowland conjured up new and electrifying sounds by looping his guitar through the system, thus creating a series of consecutive in-line effects, feedback loops and distortions. For the fist time, the band members actually enjoyed being in the studio, and an EP, 'Hee Haw', was subsequently released containing five new tracks.

Years later, Mick Harvey would say, *'After countless performances in Australia we were starting to feel as if we had completed our training. We felt strong enough to start anew – naturally in London. We really thought we'd hit the big time as soon as we got there'.* The Boys Next Door had nothing to lose by leaving Australia. They were being practically ignored by the record industry and they had been barred from playing at a number of venues. At the end of the day, the band didn't have any other choice than to uproot and head for pastures new, to try their luck in England. On 16 February 1980 The Boys Next Door played a farewell concert at the Crystal Ballroom where they handed out to their fans copies of 'Happy Birthday', a single they had produced especially for the occasion. The band decided that since they were changing continents they might as well change their name, too. 26 hours later, The Birthday Party arrived at London Heathrow. Nick is quoted to have said that he took the name from a scene from one of his favourite novels, Dostojevski's 'Crime and Punishment', where Katharina Ivanova holds a tumultuous wake for her dead husband instead of a birthday party. In actual fact the band took their new name from their song 'Happy Birthday'. More important was that, with their change of name, the Australians were hoping for a fresh start.

I listen to his records and go to his concerts.
That's the greatest compliment I can pay an artist.

Iggy Pop (1999)

What you missed in Time Out magazine last week...

Don't miss it this week.

2

London

The only good cop is a dead cop –
I hate every cop in this town.

T-shirt-print of Big Daddy Roth (Ratfink)

When The Birthday Party arrived in England on 21 February 1980, London was in the throes of depression. Margaret Thatcher, the then Prime Minister, had initiated radical policies of privatisation and reform that were having a destructive effect on the social cohesion of the country. The poor could only look on in horror as Thatcher sold off state assets and gave away the proceeds to those who had elected her, while the vast majority had to endure the acute economic recession she had triggered. The Birthday Party had chosen a bad time to settle in England. They received very little money from their parents, jobs were hard to come by, and without a return ticket home to Melbourne, they were stranded, destitute in a city where the cost of living was notoriously high. As if that was not enough, England in winter can be one of the most drab and hideous places in the world. The Australians had left home at the height of a glorious summer. The grey skies, beating rain and cutting wind that greeted them on their arrival in London were anything but inviting. The young musicians from Melbourne had naively looked forward to a promising new future in Swinging London, and although they hadn't exactly been expecting Britain to be paradise, the conditions that welcomed them were a sobering experience. They spent their first few weeks in the city at a hotel in Gloucester Road in South Kensington and were just getting used to life away from home when Rowland was robbed and Tracy had his ghettoblaster stolen. Not long after, they managed to find a one-bedroom ground floor apartment with basic amenities near Earl's Court in West London but which was clearly too small for five people. The kitchen doubled up as the lounge, and all there was to the bedroom were two camp beds. The new arrivals endeavoured to cheer themselves up by visiting the Royal Academy of Art and even took a short trip to Paris which, in Australian terms, was only a stone's throw away from the English capital. However, the general mood remained sombre. Fond memories of Rowland and Mick's bright and breezy apartment back in sun-drenched Melbourne nearly made them forget all about the narrow-minded press and ignorant audiences Down Under they had so wanted to get away from. The musicians didn't even have that in London, just this dump of a flat the dejected young men had to share. Mick was the only one to find a regular job and worked part-time at a Lyon's supermarket. Now that he could afford to rent a room of his own, he left Earl's Court to take up furnished lodgings in West Kensington. The others were glad of the extra space.

The realisation that London's streets weren't paved with gold virtually paralysed the members of The Birthday Party. All the plans they had made, the naive expectation that they could continue in London where they had left off in Melbourne, lay in tatters. Browbeaten and disillusioned, they couldn't even muster the motivation to contact the music press, never mind organise their first London concert. In March, they gathered up their dwindling personal belongings and their instruments and moved house again, this time to 39 Maxwell Road in Fulham. Though not quite the style they had been accustomed to in Australia, the Fulham flat was definitely a big improvement on the confines of Earl's Court. Because money was tight, the Australians lived on Indian takeaways which led to Rowland's being diagnosed with malnutrition. Therefore, he broke the promise he had made to himself and resolved to ask his family back home for a helping hand till things were sorted out. Writing songs and dreaming of better days held the band together during this gruelling time. They started penning new material during sessions at the new flat and wrote 'King Ink' and 'Nick the Stripper', songs that testified to Cave's artistic, multifaceted character. Nonetheless, the pressures of daily life were stifling the band members' ingenuity, as they were wasting too much of their energy trying to make ends meet and organising drugs.

April was wet and rainy and the inhabitants of Maxwell Road were having trouble coming up with the rent. As a sign of solidarity, Mick Harvey gave up the furnished room he now shared with his girlfriend, Katy Beale, and the two of them moved in with the rest of the band. Katy had just moved to London, and the couple had it relatively easy, even working in the same supermarket. They managed to distance themselves from the problems the others were facing and understanding that, in England, one day of sunshine might be followed by two weeks

of rain, Mick and Katy made the most of things, often taking refuge at the cinema when the rain showed no signs of letting up. The couple led an orderly life while the others were coming to learn to cope with adversity instead of struggling against it. Ignorant of the fact that they had a claim to social security, they muddled through, working days here and there for cash in hand. But they hadn't come to London to earn a pittance from disparaging jobs; they had come to England to make music.

Things were starting to get out of hand. Instead of sleeping all day, as pop stars should, the Australians had to get up early and arrive at the job agencies by eight, taking on jobs as dishwashers, paperboys, cleaners and even zookeepers. If there was nothing doing, they would hit the street and try again the next day. They then had the choice of either hanging around killing time or turning their attention to petty crime, something that had been part of their irreverent aura in Australia but, if truth be told, had been pure invention. Now the Australians went on the lookout for bikes they could steal and then sell on. Directing all their energies into eking out some kind of tolerable existence sounded the death knell for their creativity which, by this stage, had more or less fallen by the wayside. Nick Cave had had an initial creative outburst but had now stopped writing altogether. The rest of the band likewise failed to show any signs of venting their particular frustrations by putting them to music. At the end of a long day, all that remained was a couple of pounds in their pockets that soon disappeared: cigarettes and liquor were much more expensive in London than back home. Drugs were about the same price, but what use was that if there wasn't any hard cash left over to buy them with?

The pressures that hung over the band were getting the musicians down. Memories of the home comforts they had so taken for granted in Australia, combined with the condescending attitude of the English toward their colonial cousins from Down Under, merely served to exacerbate the situation further. In a country where people's accents were seen to reflect their social standing, the English regarded Australians as common unless they were rich and famous. Rowland and Nick reiterated in later interviews that their powerlessness to do anything about this remote, stuck-up attitude actually threatened to drive a wedge between them. Whoever showed any sign of weakness and like Phill Calvert hadn't perfected the art of emotional self-defence, fell victim to the aggression that was now inherent among the members of the band. Presenting a strong united front to the outside while masking any frailty within, is a tactic most Australians know all too well and is deeply rooted in the country's colonial past as a vast penal colony. Beset by money worries and financial interdependence, things seemed to be getting worse instead of better.

The mood improved markedly when Anita, Genevieve and Caitlin, Nick's, Rowland's and Tracy's girlfriends, arrived in London from Melbourne in May. The loneliness each of the young men had been feeling soon began to dissipate, and this happy reunion made them more confident in the cold, alien environment of this foreign metropolis. The family was together again. When Keith Glass turned up during his annual trip to London in May 1980, he was shocked at the desolate physical and mental state of his stranded protégés. Although he reproached them for having let themselves go, his arrival on the scene put The Birthday Party back on track. Glass went knocking on the doors of the record companies he was familiar with in an attempt to ascertain what the band's chances were and to find out who they could turn to arrange their first gig. The Birthday Party had brought enough material with them from Australia to cut an album, but Glass had totally misread the situation. He was forced to realise that obtaining licences via Australian record companies wasn't the way things worked in the UK. Then Glass had to leave London unexpectedly before he could make any real headway, as problems had cropped up with the lease on his record shop back in Melbourne.

The English music business was structured differently from that in Australia. The gang of four had been so convinced that it would be easy to gain a foothold in the London punk rock scene, but instead were forced to accept that they were the only band of that mould in town. Their music sounded outdated in the fast-moving, image-conscious hectic of Thatcher's England. The Sex Pistols, The Fall and The Pop Group had had their day and had been ousted by more docile bands that had merely assumed the superficial attitudes of punk while jettisoning the rest. The originals were now being hounded by the music press who knocked their music as useless and the bands themselves as charlatans. After Sex Pistol Sid Vicious's overdose in February 1979 and Joy Division's Ian Curtis's suicide in May 1980, punk was no longer regarded as a bracing form of protest or an attractive utopia, but rather as a haven for dirty and decadent drop-outs.

The Birthday Party was dismayed at this state of affairs, as punk still held a deep-rooted relevance for them, the only thing that had kept them going. They were not minded to give up on all they had worked for, as artistic suicide wasn't an option they were willing to take. But there was nothing the disappointed young men could do, other than to despise those English bands and musicians who had taken it upon themselves to spearhead the new wave onslaught. For The Birthday Party, groups like Echo & The Bunnymen, Simple Minds, The Cure, Siouxsie & The Banshees and A Certain Ratio were listless and artificial, more interested in making money than upholding their artistic integrity.

These groups saw themselves as the descendants of the English pop tradition and tried to create a sound bathed in cool perfection. The synthesizer was often the predominant instrument, and The Birthday Party felt that these bands tried too hard to remain detached from their audiences. The musicians from Australia found the new generation of English pop bands tedious and increasingly felt like lone fighters in the desolate world of English music. They saw through the socialist credentials of some of the London new wave bands which had mutated into an early form of political correctness in reaction to the ultra-conservative policies of the Tory party under Thatcher that had resulted in a vast catalogue of stringent rules of conduct. The music press, unsure of its own future in the Brave New World of Tory Britain, had gladly jumped on the bandwagon and willingly became a vehicle for a contemporary form of political protest that lacked real substance. The Australians were horrified. Nothing could have been further from The Birthday Party's musical aspirations and way of life. Punk had initially defined itself as the expression of individuality, but the political correctness of the music now being played by this new generation of English bands came across as nothing more than simple tactics.

The Birthday Party were totally indifferent to claims that the birth of new wave also marked the renaissance of the English pop song. The phalanx of groups like ABC, The Human League, Culture Club, Heaven 17 or Prefab Sprout, that flourished between 1981 and 1983 was a developement The Birthday Party managed to miss. In its heyday, punk had not only rebelled against authority and middle-class hypocrisy, but had also stood by its victims when need be. Now, the music press had turned its back on this form of youth protest and wanted nothing more to do with it. The Australians could only look on with incomprehension and disdain. They did, however, have time for Joy Division, The Pop Group and The Fall who left a lasting impression on the Australians with their blend of deep, clever black humour and their self-acclaimed emotional style. This stance explains how Joy Division, a name fraught with taboo, were able to directly refer to the brigades of Jewish prostitutes in the Nazi concentration camps without defaming the victims, willingly using Nazi symbolism without being Nazis themselves.

At the beginning of summer 1980, things started to look up for The Birthday Party. On 29 June, more than four months after their arrival in England, they played their first gig in London's Rock Garden. A week later, on Daniel Miller's invitation, they played the Moonlight Club in West Hampstead as support for the German band DAF (Deutsch Amerikanische Freundschaft). Miller, the founder of the hugely successful Mute Record label that had signed up groups like Depeche Mode, wasn't the only one The Birthday Party had impressed. Ivo Watts-Russell, head of the independent 4AD label, came to see the show and was amazed by the band's brutal stage presence, especially that of its frontman, Nick Cave. If Miller had had the funds, he would have signed up Cave and the band there and then rather than having to wait for another three years, as was the case. But he did advise his friend to give The Birthday Party a chance. Watts-Russell was fascinated by recent developments in the music scene and was one of the few outsiders who were able to appreciate The Birthday Party's artistic vision or fully understand their opposition to compromise in any form.

The Boys Next Door's Australian gigs paled into insignificance compared to the concerts The Birthday Party played in June and July of 1980 in London. They were characterised by a much more profound musical style, a belligerence in response to the superficiality of the London pop scene and their own respective frustrations. As if being in London had challenged them to clean up their act and despite their inherent savage, destructive energy, The Birthday Party was more focused, precise and vociferous than ever before. Watts-Russell, impressed by Cave's sombre stage persona, took them under contract and the first official single, 'The Friend Catcher', was released on 4AD in the UK that October. However, on their own initiative and without any outside help, The Birthday Party had previously managed to issue two singles taken from the material they had recorded during the 'Hee-Haw' sessions, 'Happy Birthday/Riddle House' and 'Mr Clarinet'. Although carried by a number of independent record shops in London, these seven-inch singles had been practically ignored by punters.

With the 4AD deal and several live performances under their belt, the BBC's star DJ, John Peel, also started taking an interest in The Birthday Party. He had stumbled across the singles that were doing the rounds in London, and soon began to feature them on his Radio 1 show. Peel invited them to do one of the internationally renowned 'Peel Sessions' which had meanwhile become something of an institution. These sessions involved bands recording and mixing four tracks in one day. And who were The Birthday Party to turn such an offer down? When they went into the studio and recorded 'King Ink', 'Cry', 'Yard', and 'Figure of Fun', John Peel was visibly impressed. The songs confirmed his faith in the band and he regularly aired them on his show. In November 1980, Watts-Russell, encouraged by the reaction the Australians were getting, decided to issue The Birthday Party's first British album, under licence from Missing Link, the Australian record company that pulled the strings.

This was a ray of hope for the band. More and more people were starting to take notice, especially due to the airplay given to their songs on the hugely popular John Peel show. 'The Friend Catcher' even jumped to number 3 in the English independent charts for a short time in the spring of 1981. But, the Australians were disappointed with the reaction of audiences to their concerts. Their live performances were as on-key, energetic and as professional as ever, but English audiences, more used to new wave codes and conventions, were unable to show much grasp of what the shows were all about. The reactions of the big music magazines were also surprisingly reserved. Indeed, they couldn't avoid the fact that The Birthday Party was in their faces, even though they were late arrivals on the English music scene, but they politely declined to dedicate any comprehensive coverage to this new phenomenon. Nevertheless, the group, reunited in body and soul, flew back to Melbourne in November 1980 to play a series of concerts there and to visit their families. Many back home had been wondering what had become of The Boys Next Door during their ten-month absence from their homeland, so it was much to everybody's surprise when the band, in its new incarnation as The Birthday Party, presented itself as a rock-solid unit to its audiences back home. It seemed like they had had to turn their backs on their native land with all the courage it had taken them to set off into the bright blue yonder for Australian audiences to relish their concerts as a sensation not to be missed. Fans, including INXS's Michael Hutchence, a great admirer of the band, had to queue around the block to get in to see them at the Crystal Ballroom on New Year's Eve 1980. The band were flattered but reacted to all the hype with a sense of irritation, their shows in Sydney, Adelaide and Melbourne marked by the usual verbal abuse and confrontation. Nick Cave and the others were irked by the fickleness of these audiences who had once despised them. It seemed that absence did make the heart grow fonder, after all. The Birthday Party had become accustomed to playing in front of more passive London audiences, so their gigs were all the more deafening and liable to get out of hand, even at the bigger venues. Nothing seemed to be beyond the young raging musicians on stage. Tracy Pew, lost in the heat of the moment, even managed to push a fan off the stage at the Crystal Ballroom, breaking his ribs in the process. The band also used their time in Melbourne at the turn of the year to record their first regular album, 'Prayers On Fire', although Missing Link had just released an album entitled 'The Boys Next Door'. The Boys Next Who? This particular album featured a compilation of songs that The Boys Next Door had recorded at various stages of their career and included the singles 'The Friend Catcher', 'Riddle House', and 'Happy Birthday', as well as some previously unreleased material from the Hee-Haw sessions. Its release eventually led to a fall-out between Nick Cave and Keith Glass. Glass had issued the album on his own initiative, so here was The Birthday Party on a promotion tour of Australia where a record was doing the rounds with the wrong name on the label and a sleeve Glass had designed without asking. There didn't seem to be much logic to that, but what could the band do? Open their mouths and risk missing out on the imminent recording session?

Around about the same time, the band members came to realise that they really could get audiences going, leaving behind an impression on them that was uplifting. The Birthday Party had never sensed that reaction before. Australian fans regarded the band as a loud, disreputable, energy-laden self-annihilating powerhouse, stronger than the audience itself. Tracy's brutal, omnipresent bass guitar and Nick's never-tiring attempts at getting fans to participate in the show by hurling insults at them, talking to them, and demanding at the top of his voice that they show some kind of reaction, were something audiences, for their part, had never before experienced. This mood continued during the recording sessions for the new album. The familiar easygoing atmosphere at Armstrong's Audio and Visual Studios in Melbourne was heightened by the frequent visits of friends and acquaintances, and the sessions usually turned into typically Australian drinking binges. The album profited greatly from this unperturbed, relaxed atmosphere. The utterly sarcastic self-reflexive song, 'Nick The Stripper', with its famous lines *'Nick the stripper, hideous to the eye, he's a fat little insect, here we go again'* was selected by Keith Glass and the group as a single off 'Prayers On Fire' and a video shoot was scheduled for the day before the band was due to return to London. The Rich Kids, the same team of directors who had produced the video for 'Shivers' two years previously, were contracted to work on this one, too. John Hillcoat, who would receive international tributes for his critically acclaimed movie 'Ghosts of the Civil Dead' ten years later, was also part of the team for the first time.

Hillcoat and The Rich Kids announced the date of the shoot publicly and declared that if anybody wanted to be an extra, they should turn up at a particular rubbish dump the city had commissioned but not yet used. The video was to pay homage to the surrealist Italian director, Frederico Fellini, famed for his movies 'Satyricon' and 'Casanova'. Although laconically labelled 'Carnival in Hell', the shoot promptly turned into an unforgettable huge going-away party for The Birthday Party. Several hundred fans turned up in magnificent fancy dress, armed with generous amounts of alcohol and illicit drugs and turned the site into an imposing backdrop for a memorable happening. Everybody was as high as a kite and no-one could have failed to enjoy the atmosphere.

Tracy wore a cowboy hat during filming, a bit like Dennis Hopper's Stetson in Wim Wenders's movie 'The American Friend'. He never took it off again. Tracy wore the hat with a net shirt at the first concert The Birthday Party played on 18 March

1981 back in London and looked like one of the infamous Village People, an urban cowboy with overtly gay undertones. This was typical of the band's sense of humour. As one of The Boys Next Door, Tracy used to paint on a false Hitler moustache and now, here he was, the main character in a completely different kind of masquerade. Invigorated by the support the band had encountered in Melbourne, The Birthday Party pretentiously started to act like the stars they had yet to become. The band's live performances were grandiose, whether they were the main act or on a double bill with other groups. They were on the threshold to stardom, not quite there yet, and used this phase in their development as a practice ground on that rocky path from being simple unknowns to becoming legends. Suddenly, the negative and derisive reactions they had been getting in England turned around and they were now being accepted as a proud and talented band, albeit with an aura of danger and self-confident arrogance. London audiences slowly started to realise that The Birthday Party was a group to be taken seriously.

The band's concerts were now a more regular event in the London calendar. Bigger audiences and the advent of more positive coverage in the English press notably validated Nick Cave's conviction that he was indeed a rock star. But it wasn't just his on-stage persona that was attracting the attention of the public and critics alike. The band had at last fine-tuned their act without throwing their manic and unpredictable style overboard. No-one could now overlook that fact. Their concerts were received as a chaotic mixed bag of violent outbursts, and Nick was in his element tormenting people in the front rows. Rowland created loud feedback loops on his electric guitar, Mick, opposite him, just as impressive, torturing the strings of his own instrument, pushing it to the limits. Accompanying them, Tracy, drunk as ever, thumping out his bass, his stage persona menacing as he played, while Phill's perfectly synchronous drumming rounded the set off. Here was a band that was prepared to steadfastly uphold its own principles and blatantly parade its deep-rooted convictions. It incorporated them in a show of physically demanding self-confidence, never lowering its sights.

Despite all these promising developments, Nick Cave was having a hard time with the English music press. Cave was abusive and quite undiplomatic during interviews and didn't shy back from upsetting his fans. He reacted heatedly and with consternation whenever journalists, constantly would attempt to compare The Birthday Party to other groups such as Pere Ubu or Cpt. Beefheart – but who could blame them. Nick didn't make any friends during this time of anxious cause and effect, although 'Prayers On Fire' had been received positively by critics after its release in England in April 1981. The apparent contradictory reactions of the monopolistic English music press did

follow a certain internal logic, however. They didn't want to get involved with The Birthday Party, but they couldn't totally turn a blind eye to the band either. Cave and the press were mutually suspicious, and neither his comments that English fans were like a herd of sheep nor the media's preposterous allegation that The Birthday Party were politically active supporters of Aborigine rights could calm things down. All that remained were the band's music and live performances which bore out that The Birthday Party was undeniably making the grade, despite the vexation the media was causing them.

The band picked up steam in 1981 and was able to put to good use the experience they had gained from a benefit concert they had played at the Crystal Ballroom the previous December. John Peel invited them back into the studio and The Birthday Party played a set which comprised cover versions of some of the dirtiest and hardest Stooges songs, '1969', 'Funhouse', 'I wanna be your dog', and 'Loose'. The latter was destined to become the highlight of the session and, at the same time, came to epitomise the band's newer, sharper sound. 'Release the Bats', also recorded for the first time during the Peel Sessions, mutated into an anthem for the Gothic faction at The Birthday Party's concerts. The band had composed 'Release the Bats' as biting irony set to music, but the Gothic contingency failed to see the funny side. How could they have guessed that they were the victims of a wind-up when Cave used to turn up on stage with his hair dyed jet-black and his eyes ringed with mascara, sporting a crucifix? Nick Cave had to get used to announcing, *'the next song is the song you love the most but we hate the most'*, every time the band was about to play it – before eventually deciding to delete it from their repertoire forever.

Nick didn't have much opportunity to see the funny side of life himself during the band's first tour of England in June 1981 as support for new wave band Bauhaus, like The Birthday Party under contract with 4AD. Bauhaus's videos alluded to a grim fixation on death and dark bat-imagery with an outstanding black-and-white approach reminiscent of the horror genre of the 20s and 30s, although the group did have its finger firmly on the pulse of the 80s. They knew what their audiences expected, and Peter Murphy's dramatic persona was a manifestation fans could readily identify with. The Australians got on well enough with Bauhaus during the tour but were none too pleased when The Birthday Party's music and style started appealing to their fans, so they were glad when the tour ended on 25 June. Nick Cave and Rowland S. Howard wrote The Birthday Party's songs which were becoming rather complex, much more so than Bau-haus' material. Most of the bands that were defining the English music scene at that time didn't have a look-in. The Birthday

Party's music was set in heavily fragmented acoustic anthologies of sound-walls, and their songs were rooted in the blues and the dark, heavy monotones of American punk rock. 'Prayers On Fire' was galvanised by Tracy Pew's dominant bass and the thumping beats of Phill Calvert's drums. Mick Harvey's guitar and Rowland S. Howard's awesome atonal quality enhanced the texture of the entire album, while Nick Cave's lyrics were an abstraction in the face of the formidable energy of the music that plunged it into existential sparseness. This unity was entrenched in the reality that showing vulnerability or emotion was seen as a weakness that didn't fit in with The Birthday Party's all too masculine philosophy. Nick Cave always wrote his lyrics along the same lines, which also served to keep a sense of balance within the group: If you fuck around with me, I'll fuck you twice.

During the recording of 'Prayer's On Fire', Nick Cave started to perfect his singing, consequently appearing older than he really was. His vocals took on a darker and more mysterious timbre, sometimes even bordering on the pretentious, a progression that was becoming increasingly apparent with every recording he made. In combination with the brutal lamenting music of the band, Cave's vocals came over as anything but friendly. After a while, this sound was instantly identifiable as his trademark. As if he was following in the footsteps of Screamin' Jay Hawkins whose classic 'I'll Put a Spell on You' belonged to The Birthday Party's repertoire, Nick sang, hissed and screamed out his lyrics like a detached, frenetic nightmarish testimony over the multi-layered, ear-splitting music of the band behind him. His fantasies of alienation take on an exaggerated imagery of decadence and madness. The lines *'King Ink Wake up wake up, up, up, up, a bug crawls up the wall, King Ink feels like a bug and he hates his rotten shell'*, inspired by Kafka's 'The Transformation', are a classic document to the quality of Cave's vocals on 'Prayers Of Fire'. In the lines *'Sand and soot and dust and dirt dirt dirt dirt, King Ink feels like a bug swimming in a soup bowl'*, Nick Cave alludes to a life spent in filth suffering from serious personality disorders. In The Birthday Party's classic 'Zoo Music Girl' he describes his relationship with Anita Lane in a flash of personal revelation. Cave sings *'Our life together is a hollow tooth'*, only to ascertain a little further on *'If there is one thing I desire in the world is to make love to my Zoo Music Girl (...) Oh God! Please let me die beneath her fists'*. In interviews, Cave has often stated that the songs he wrote in 1980 and 1981 were penned while he was under the influence and that he often woke up around midday to discover he had a fragment of a song in his pocket, although he couldn't remember writing it. It is fascinating how Cave instinctively knew – or was it down to the alcohol? – how to hide his feelings behind a wall of detached drollness. He spoke the words his fans wanted to hear, showing them a truth in an encoded manifest, totally unlike the romantically sweet and politically premeditated communication of other more mainstream bands who were adorning the covers of the big magazines at that time. It was a deep nihilistic sense of humour, an Australian form of sarcasm and wit, that differentiated The Birthday Party from its peers. Unlike the dogmatic and frequently commercially compromised performances of 'the others', The Birthday Party kept a healthy distance between themselves and the impressions they left on their audiences. All the dirt and filthy language in Nick's lyrics were the sustenance he took along on this new excursion into unfamiliar territory, a fantasy world full of the kind of wit and humour the band members could fully appreciate.

On 22 September 1982, The Birthday Party headed off to the USA to play a few gigs in New York and a couple of North Eastern cities that they had been offered at short notice. Two shows in New York's Underground Club and the Ritz were enough for the organisers to cancel the two remaining sets. The band had come across as posing an uncalculated risk the organisers now felt they couldn't take. Had anything happened to warrant that kind of reaction? Well, Nick had tried to strangle a woman with his microphone lead at the Underground Club, and Mick, drunk and jet-lagged, had called the audience bastards. At the Ritz, Nick purposely split his own head open on the drumset, hoping the concert would be cancelled. He later said: *'We didn't do anything to deserve a reaction like that. Our concert at the Ritz was rather low-key. They stopped the show and told us that if we didn't piss off before the DJ played his second record, we wouldn't get paid. So, we took the money and ran'*. After that fiasco, the band spent a week hanging out in New York, had another gig to look forward to, and met the American rock singer and extreme performance artist, Lydia Lunch. Since her friends had given her 'Prayers On Fire' as a present, Lunch was a big fan of the band. She was especially impressed by its lead singer, never suspecting that the two of them would soon become friends and work on a number of projects together.

America was in many ways an irritating experience for the Australians. On the one hand, they had managed to set foot in the Big Apple, the capital of the world, the birthplace of contemporary music, which had drawn its artistic consciousness from a deliberate disregard for taboos and inhibitions. New York was also home to The Velvet Underground, Lou Reed and Bob Dylan. Conversely, the band realised that New York was much less up-front, not nearly as tolerant, self-effacing, or provocative as elsewhere. They were clearly confronted with audiences who were unable to comprehend what The Birthday Party was about. Long before stage-diving and mosh pits became an integral part of American punk, hip-hop and heavy metal concerts, Nick

would dive straight into the audience and didn't give a damn whether he broke a bone or two. He sometimes raised his hands, and in Chicago even unabashedly demanded that the audience 'throw drugs on to the stage!' And they did. They didn't know what had hit them.

Back in London, The Birthday Party realised that time was on their side. They played Brixton for the first time, surrounded by over 1000 adoring fans, and doors were opening all over the place. Their stage shows gave audiences exactly what they wanted, but somehow, the musicians sensed that in doing so, they were losing much of the freedom they had always exuded and were running the risk of becoming caricatures. And it hurt. After two years in exile, The Birthday Party could now look forward to a relatively cosy life, free of financial worries but with a much more mainstream appeal. A price they couldn't afford to pay. But this also meant that they would have to bolster their newly-found musical expression, consolidation necessary so as not to put the musicians' currant material situation at risk. The Birthday Party reacted to what they saw as 'harmony got out of control' with an instinctive violence towards each other and an attempt to destabilise the band from within. Their concerts in Germany, Holland, Switzerland and Italy in November were marked by conscious efforts to instil some level of unpredictability into their performances and emphasised the band's true raison d'être. As documented on various bootlegs and tapes circulated later, The Birthday Party was, without a doubt, the most raucous band of the era.

There were whispers in the boardrooms of some of the big international record companies around December 1981 that there was a band out there, quite unlike the rest: Rougher, angrier, more aloof and full of themselves – and with a faithful fan base. Chris Carr, an English journalist, had been trying to come up with business and media contacts for Nick and his friends and thought it might be a prudent idea to invite some record label bigwigs to the band's concert on 11 December 1981 at the Central London Poly Club. The Australians, fully aware that there were VIPs in the audience, got rat-arsed on the booze the organisers had bought in for the after-show knees-up. The gig ended in a chaotic brawl and left Mick especially at a complete loss and totally pissed off. This wasn't the first Birthday Party gig that had got out of control, but this time the music had also been a disaster. Tracy could barely concentrate on playing after a heroin overdose and kept on falling flat on his face. This wasn't quite what they had had in mind as a united front. It had come to the stage that the band was ready to self-destruct, a tragedy that caused the record company managers leaving the concert in disgust, of the opinion that this band was totally unpredictable – and therefore unmarketable. The Birthday Party had no idea where to go next. What were they to do if all

they could manage was to consciously sabotage their act? What would happen if an all-encompassing nihilism destabilised their creativity once and for all? Confusion and unabashed fury at each other accompanied the band on an inter-continental flight back to Melbourne where, like the previous year, they were to record an album and play a series of concerts. At least the sun always shone down on Australia.

If anybody on the bus dared to open their mouth when Amazing Grace was on, Nick Cave would give them a thick ear. That's why I'll never forget the words:

*Amazing grace! How sweet the sound
That saved a wretch like me
I once was lost, but now am found
Was blind, but now I see*

*'Twas grace that taught my heart to fear
And grace my fears relieved
How precious did that grace appear
The hour I first believed*

*Through many dangers, toils and snares
I have already come
'Tis grace hath brought me safe thus far
And grace will lead me home*

*The Lord has promised good to me
His Word my hope secures
He will my shield and portion be
As long as life endures*

*Yea, when this flesh and heart shall fail
And mortal life shall cease
I shall possess, within the veil
A life of joy and peace*

*The world shall soon dissolve like snow
The sun refuse to shine
But God, who called me here below
Shall be forever mine*

*When we've been there ten thousand years
Bright shining as the sun
We've no less days to sing God's praise
Than when we'd first begun*

Alexander Hacke *(Einstürzende Neubauten)*

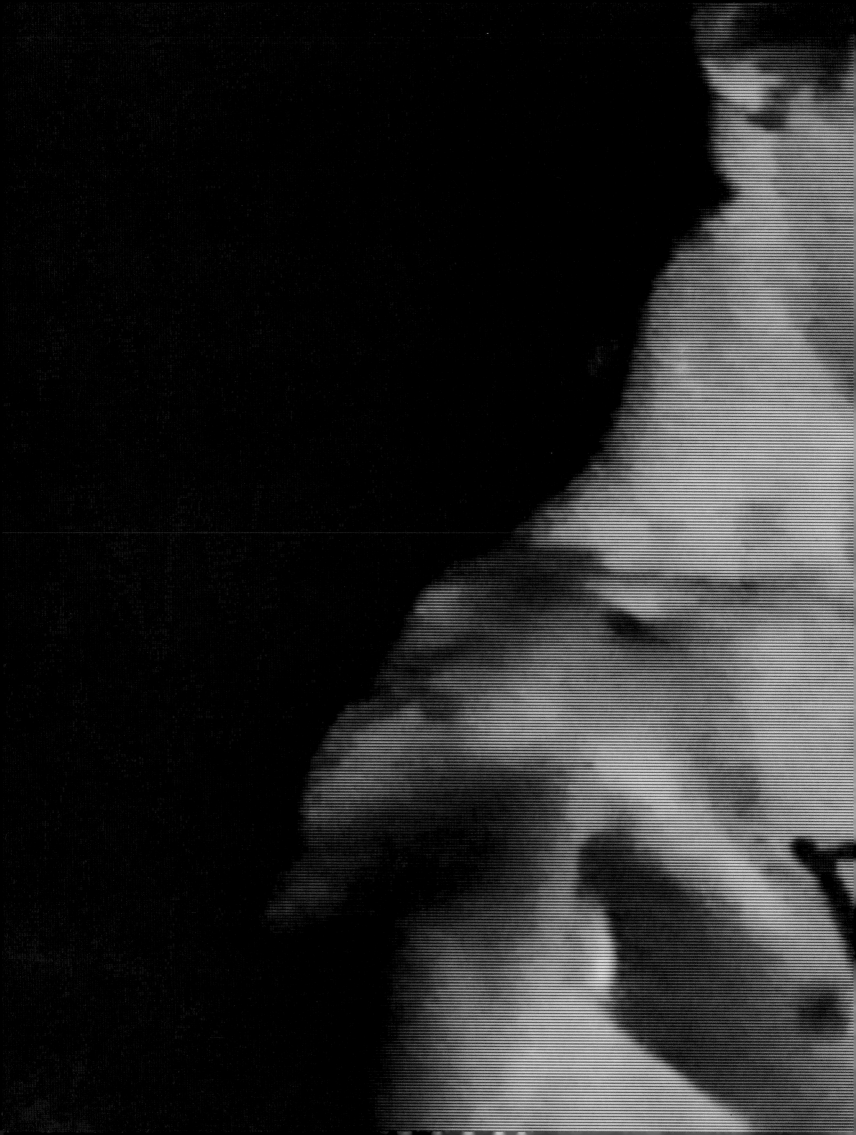

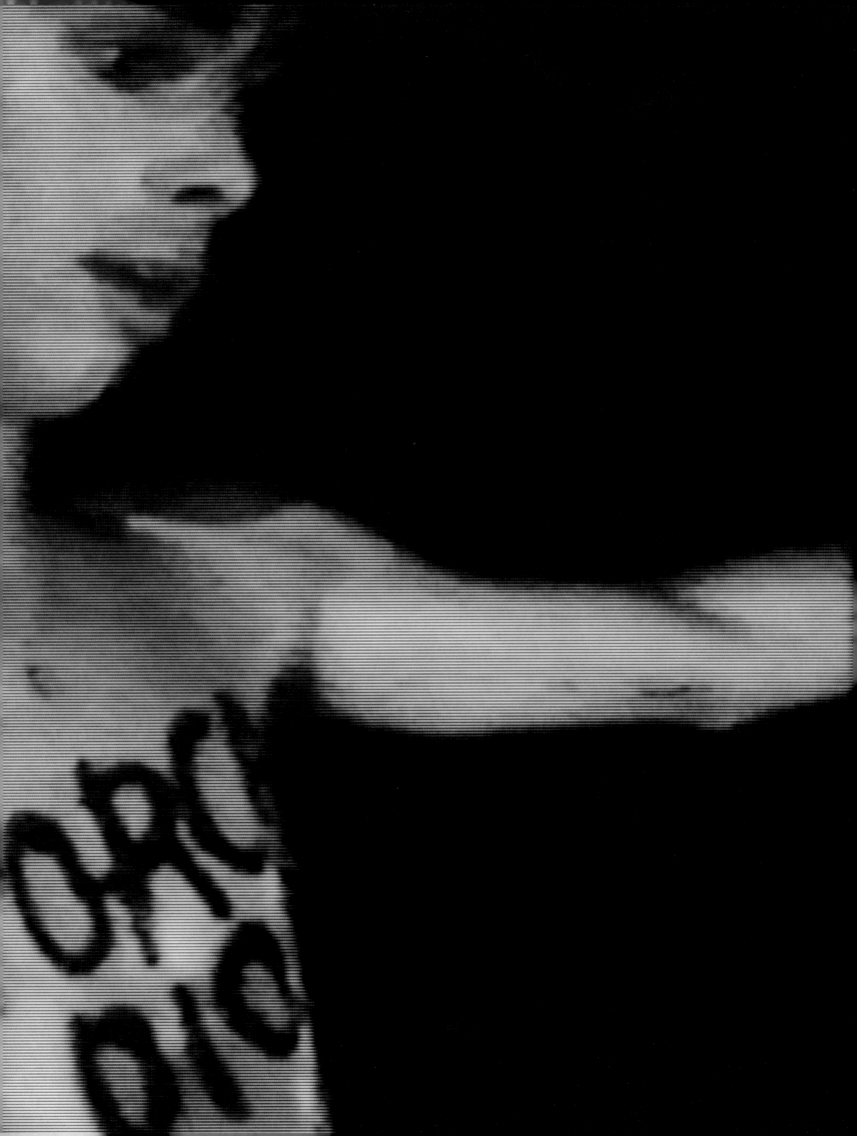

Junk

I saw a shooting star tonight / And I thought of you

Bob Dylan, „Shooting Star"

One of the foremost distinguishing attributes of rock music penned by artists who haven't just experimented with hard drugs like heroin but who, at some stage in their lives, have been physically and mentally addicted, is the equanimity that invariably comes with a drug-taking lifestyle. The music of a long list of legendary artists from Miles Davis to John Lennon appears more succinct and intricate than that of musicians who never envisaged messing around with illegal substances. The impact of heroin on how they express their art has been well documented throughout the entire history of rock music. To begin with, many aspects of everyday life simply start to appear trivial. Heroin, essentially a powerful analgesic, elevates the user to a different plane of consciousness while expanding the mind and confounding the senses. It improves concentration and, for as long as its effects are felt, users believe that everything in the universe revolves around them. Steadfastly convinced of their invincibility and unimpeded by convention, artists become more assertive in expressing their talents. The uninitiated, however, consider heroin users as totally self-involved, as far removed from their brand of reality as anyone can get. On the other hand, fans look up to celebrity users with a sense of awe, their glamorous stage personas full of the vitality of youth. The impelling force to be creative heroin induces in people frequently results in an overpowering temptation to prolong the sensation of being outwith the real world. But as everyone knows, living in a state of heroin-induced euphoria for too long soon leads to addiction proper. Moreover, once the craving sets in, users will risk anything to get a hit. If impure or mixed with other substances heroin can lead to a fatal overdose, addicts' bodies ravaged by the increasing amounts of poison put into them. Most users do learn to live with this risk and tend to play it down. Celebrity heroin addicts have a further worry to contend with. Their predilection for the drug is often common knowledge, so fans may view their lifestyles as perfectly acceptable alternatives to their own dull realities and might then choose to emulate them. For years, Nick Cave was disparaged by the English press for making drug-taking appear innocuous. His having to answer to slurs that he was a poor role model and was to blame for much copycat behaviour eventually became more important to the media than The Birthday Party's music. It didn't seem to occur to anyone that addictions are a purely private matter first and foremost – and any journalist who ignores the complexity of the problem and tries to moralise from the pulpit of so-called decency all too often runs the risk of playing it down in a narrow black and white superficiality.

Nick Cave, Rowland S. Howard, and Tracy Pew soon realised that heroin had a welcome side effect that enabled the band to secure an unassailable position from which its members could act on instinct and without reserve. Even Phill and Mick were wrapped up in the mystery of the drug, although they themselves didn't use it. In retrospect, heroin was an inherent part of The Birthday Party's self-image, a balancing act between an addiction to pleasure and a compulsion to provoke. Consequently, The Birthday Party's sound was much more fierce and distinct from that of the more temperate bands of the day. The band was as much an expression of male bonding as it was the summit of an existentialist lifestyle defined by a push for individual freedom. Ruthless if need be, refusing to bow to precedent, The Birthday Party was symbolic of a system of values that also remained valid offstage when its members had returned to the constraints of everyday life. The musicians had created a little Australian enclave in England, along with their girlfriends, a clique outsiders found hard to infiltrate. Many – like Lydia Lunch – who refused to yield to the temptation of hard drugs, still felt drawn to The Birthday Party and took strength from living a life free of responsibility towards others. Nick Cave, Mick Harvey, and the rest of the band defined themselves through the intangible values of pride, independence, and inner force both within and without their circle. The Birthday Party's music was an expression of faith and therefore much more important to them than fame or riches. It was firmly rooted in the existentialist experience the band members were consciously seeking, reflected in the challenges they felt they

would always be in a position to rise to. That this was an equation with a variety of unknown variables, fuelled by drugs and the audacity of youth, was an irrefutable fact of life. So they lived for the day, convinced that growing old was something that would never happen to them.

The four musicians saw the studio sessions The Birthday Party had attended in Melbourne in January 1982 as a conscious expedition into pain. If their suffering got out of hand, they had the perfect tool for putting the lid back on. The band wanted to turn the new album, befittingly entitled 'Junkyard', into an acoustic flight of fancy, with a harder sound than any of their previous work and more so than 'Prayers Of Fire' had been. Melbourne's AAV-Studios lent themselves perfectly to the task, so, along with their producer, Tony Cohen, The Birthday Party started experimenting with distortions and extreme volume levels to see what they could use to best effect. The individual songs on 'Junkyard' and the stories they tell were conceived to have an intense impact on the listener, too. Nick was captivated by the bloodthirsty brutality of the Old Testament and loved old blues records that recounted the tragic lives of their broken-spirited composers, especially Robert Johnson and Leadbelly. Nick and the rest of the band went out of their way to define a point of no return with the album, to document how they had overcome their previous thresholds to establish a new, much higher tolerance level for the pain they were now expressing in their music. Cave stated in various interviews that he wanted to write songs that evoked the same profound sense of melancholy as the blues records that had left such a lasting impression on him. The soul-searching that had served as so much inspiration couldn't go on forever, so the band felt an instinctive compulsion to set to and finish 'Junkyard' before they reached breaking point.

During the recording sessions for 'Junkyard', The Birthday Party managed to evoke a mood of violence that bordered on the spiritual and deconstructed the sum of the set pieces their sound had consisted of up to then, thus purging their past of its demons. Songs like 'Nick the Stripper', 'Capers' and 'Ho-Ho' on 'Prayers Of Fire', recorded at the same location a year previously, had an evident blues feel to them. 'Junkyard' took this even further, but with a more abstract approach, the tracks stripped down into distinct individual elements and subsequently reconstructed, without ever losing any of their blues feel. 'Junkyard' depicts the world as a rat hole, a world sacked by drugs on all sides. In the song 'Hamlet (Pow, Pow, Pow)', Shakespeare's figure is portrayed as impelled in his actions by the same forces that motivate a dope fiend. Nick Cave, against a powerful bass riff, sings of *'Hamlet fishin' in the grave, thru the custard bones and stuff, he ain't got no friend in there, I believe our man's in love, Hamlet got a gun now'*, accompanied by Howard's heavily distorted guitar. It is not difficult to interpret lyrics like these as drug metaphors. *'Hamlet moves so beautiful, walking thru the flowers.'* Finally, *'Is this love? Is this love? He shoot it inside, don't let 'em steal your heart away, he went and stole my heart, hey, hey, hey.'* It is hard to imagine 'Junkyard' with its trance-like ardour, its surreal lyrics and its in-your-face screwed-up sound being penned by somebody with no experience of heroin.

The lyrics on 'Junkyard', mainly written in the studio during the recording sessions of January 1982, are direct, confrontational, and extreme. The stories they tell recount crimes of passion ('Six-Inch-Gold-Blade') and car accidents ('Dead Joe'), they repeatedly allude to filth and deformation, and evoke the valour inherent in fighting adversity in a heinous world. 'Junkyard', the title track, is a breathless depiction of an out-of-control perception of the world that illustrates the loss of innocence and morality in a ficticious story of a prostitute. *'Honey, honey, honey, honey – come on and kiss me (…) Drink to me! (…) Hack this heavenly body (…) Scratch, scrape, scratch this winning skin.'* Influences from the early days of the Lounge Lizards when Arto Lindsay was still a member are palpable in the song 'Big-Jesus-Trash-Can' with its dusky jazz moods and the way the sax comes in a moment of discord. This track perfectly illustrates how the band was able to put itself across, a prime example of critical sophistication. Nick Cave combines motifs from American road movies with a facetious depiction of his 'Big Jesus': *'(He) wears a suit of gold, (He) drives great holy tanks of gold, (He) screams from Heaven's graveyard.'* Mick Harvey had written the music to 'Big-Jesus-Trash-Can' while he was living with Jim Thirlwell in London. The two of them had undertaken a journey of discovery into the soundtracks to film noir movies and the electric jazz of Miles Davis's 'Agharta/Pangaea' period. Davis had recorded these two albums in one single day and subsequently hung up his hat for six years dedicating himself instead to heroin. Harvey was now slowly developing into the driving force behind the complex make-up of the band. Arguments had often broken out between him and Phill during the recording of the new album, especially whenever Mick was able to put his musical concepts into a more tangible and ambitious form than Phill could ever have thought possible. These artistic differences resulted in two tracks being recorded with Mick on drums instead of Phill, but such is life. True to form, The Birthday Party compensated for all this animosity by pigging out on drugs and alcohol. The band set up camp in the freshly reno-

vated studios, which, at that time, were mainly used for recording commercials. Many of the tracks on 'Junkyard' were laid down during all-nighters after the band had played gigs in Melbourne, so as to inject the surplus euphoria of these live performances into their studio work.

While The Birthday Party were in Australia, they played a total of thirteen gigs in Melbourne, Sidney, Adelaide, and Brisbane and thus embarked upon a journey into their own pasts. The fact that they had made a name for themselves in England hadn't gone unnoticed by the Australian media. The Birthday Party was suddenly featured on the cover of Rock Australia Magazine ('The Return and Revenge of The Birthday Party') and the band members were now being feted as stars, despite the air of self-irony and derision they still exuded. Fans had begun to spin legends about them and were awe-struck by how four homeboys had found fame and fortune so far from the land of their birth. The news that Nick Cave had come home to visit didn't take long to reach even the furthest flung regions of the country and the band played sell-out concerts at bigger venues than they had been used to in the past, sometimes for a series of gigs over several nights. The Birthday Party, however, were furious at being seen as prodigal sons returned home and regarded these ovations as the epitome of middle-class hypocrisy. They had moved on from the experiments in sound they had once toyed with and had found pastures new, no longer in tune with the expectations of their audiences. The situation was absurd. At concerts, fans roared and applauded before the band had even played their first note, people still expected Nick Cave to dive into the first row and create bedlam. All that this did, however, was to create chaos, the band horrified at these voyeuristic tendencies. Things had gotten so out of hand that many in Australia had come to revere Nick Cave as a kind of Antichrist, a rock star obsessed by death, a shooting star ready to burn out, a Prince of Darkness. His raven-black hair and his addiction to heroin were attributes they felt they could emulate, the multi-layered meanings in his lyrics understood as an exorbitant matrix of the answers they were seeking. These fans weren't really interested in the band's artistic development and, instead, projected their own cryptic view of the world on to its lead singer. The Birthday Party surmised this reverence as blatant ignorance and soon refused downright to deliver the myths fans like these demanded of them. The four band members were running scared that they would lose everything they had ever worked towards, so in February 1982 The Birthday Party hurled a sombre, ominous, ear-splitting wall of sound at their audiences, defending their own artistic definition: Music first, nothing else matters!

Birthday boy goes to jail

Internationally acclaimed Melbourne rock band The Birthday Party have cancelled an American and German tour - because bass guitarist Tracey Pew has been jailed for eight months.

Pew, 24, was ordered to serve four months of the sentence before becoming eligible for parole. The former Caulfield Grammar student was jailed for four months when he pleaded guilty in Prahran Court to his fourth drunk driving charge.

Police told the court that when Pew was arrested for having exceeded .05 early on January 17 he gave the name of Peter James Sutcliffe - the Yorkshire Ripper.

Messrs. John Head and J. Austin, J.P.'s also disqualified Pew from driving for five years.

Pew, of Trevor Court, Mt. Waverley, also pleaded guilty to stealing a sewing machine and clothes worth about $450 from the National Theatre, St. Kilda on December 1st, 1979. And he also pleaded guilty to stealing rice and frankfurts from a supermarket on August 13, 1979.

The court ordered that the jail sentences imposed on the theft charges be served concurrently with the four months sentence on the drunk driving charge.

Birthday Party manager Keith Glass said the band was scheduled to perform in San Francisco and Germany to promote their fourth album, *Drunk On The Pope's Blood*.

"They were originally booked to appear in San Francisco with the Dead Kennedys" Glass said "Now all that has been cancelled. We have also cancelled some German concerts".

Glass said that Barry Adamson, bassist for the well known but defunct English band, Magazine, would replace Pew in The Birthday Party.

"We hope to have him ready to appear with the band in England next month," Glass said. "We already have advance orders for 10,000 copies of the album in England."

Glass said Pew had been advised by his lawyer not to appeal against the jail sentence.

The relationship between Nick Cave and his fans had developed into something of a misunderstanding. Cave's sensitive nature and his refusal or inability to live an ordered life allowed him to hide behind a smokescreen. He saw his music as much, much more than simple entertainment, as many of his fans did, and the punk-rock blues The Birthday Party personified enabled him to over-exaggerate the point that the band was different. So he persevered, giving over-the-top stage performances that offered him a platform for his literary cut-ups, junk fantasies, and his desire for absolution. Musically, the band had done their fans a favour by not bowing to pressure. Influenced by the work they were doing on the album, dirty jazz-like elements were now beginning to take root in The Birthday Party's songs. This period of constant rowing about where the band was heading saw Mick Harvey, who had developed into a significant prime mover within the band in the meantime, and Nick Cave, lead singer and main point of contact for their audiences, finally found common ground. This unleashed previously untold synergies to create a new, more complex artistic vision.

Late in the evening of 17 January, the band was thrown into turmoil. The Birthday Party minus Phill performing as 'The Cavemen' had just played a gig in Richmond to commemorate the tenth anniversary of the Missing Link Record store along with Robert Forster, Grant McLennan, and Lindy Morrison of the Go-Betweens. After the show Tracy Pew, worse the wear for drink, had taken the wheel of his car and driven into the night with two of his mates. He was stopped by the police in a car park, taken into custody, and locked up in a cell to dry out. When asked for his particulars, Tracy gave the police the name of the Yorkshire Ripper which made them suspicious, but when they checked his story out, it came to their notice that he had previously been fined for four other petty offences, one of them stealing a sewing machine. He was sentenced to eight months in jail, starting immediately. So, Chris Walsh, an old friend of the band who had taught Tracy to play bass and who, at Caulfield, had introduced Nick to the world of the great country and western stars of yore, Merle Haggard, Johnny Cash, Leadbelly and Hank Williams, filled in for him and played the final two concerts in Australia at the Seaview Ballroom in Melbourne on 19 and 20 February 1982. While Tracy was coming to appreciate the benefits of living on an open Health Farm for recovering alcoholics and drug addicts, admitting to being clean for the first time in years and enjoying it too, the band was forced to cancel a series of gigs in San Francisco and Germany and flew back to England at the end of the month. The task that was awaiting them was to sit down and put their heads together and come up with some kind of plan on how to proceed.

Back in London, the band's routine was dictated by unfinished business. Due to Tracy's arrest back in Australia, they hadn't managed to finish recording 'Junkyard' and AVV-Studios had barred them for life, anyway. The album would now have to be completed in London and somebody still had to be found to take Tracy's place. On top of all that, a new EP was due to be released in February with the heretical title 'Drunk on the Pope's Blood' and a series of gigs in London and the English provinces was scheduled for March and April. Chris Walsh, who had stood in for Tracy back home, had stayed behind in Australia, so The Birthday Party now teamed up with Barry Adamson, the former bass player in the group Magazine. Adamson came from Moss Side, one of the roughest areas in Manchester that was notorious for its street crime and drug-related problems. He had been a friend of the band since the time of their first gigs in the London club scene in 1980 and was just as hard-boiled as they were. Their mutual respect and friendship were based on the fact that Barry, Nick, and Mick shared the same sense of black humour, although he wasn't Australian or into punk. His remarkable skill on bass, however, is unmistakable on the track 'Kiss me Black", a performance which, two years later, would be instrumental in both Nick Cave and Mick Harvey's decision to choose him as one of the founding members of The Bad Seeds. When The Birthday Party finished its English tour, Tracy, released after four months from his stint in prison, his conduct having been impeccable, rejoined the band at the end of May.

Before that, though, 4AD, The Birthday Party's English label, released the 'Drunk on the Pope's Blood' EP, which had been remixed by Tony Cohen and the band in Australia during the summer. The title had been originally picked to promote the first Boys Next Door album, but Keith Glass thought it might provoke too negative a reaction in conservative Australia, so it was ditched. 'Drunk on the Pope's Blood' was a so-called split 12-inch single and contained a performance by Lydia Lunch on the B-side entitled 'The Agony is the Ecstasy' The A-side comprised four live Birthday Party tracks with the epithet '16 Minutes of Sheer Hell.' These tracks, 'Pleasure Heads', 'King Ink', 'Zoo Music Girl' and a cover version of the Stooges' 'Loose' were taken from a live gig at The Venue in London in November 1982. However, the songs don't quite manage to convey the full vigour of the destructive energy the band's live performances were renowned for, although it is still a reasonable representation of the band's sound. Cohen and Harvey had mixed duff notes and heckling from the audience extra-loud into the recording which somehow perverts the enjoyment of listening to it. Moreover, live recordings can never substitute actually being at a gig no matter how good they are. In 1982 The Birthday Party would never have permitted the release of a mainstream live album, anyway, as these were seen as relicts of a different age, the dark 70s, a time when bands like Yes, Genesis or Deep Purple released pompous double or even triple live LPs as a kind of self-adulation, something the punk scene utterly abhorred. All the same, 'Drunk on the Pope's Blood' was an attempt to dissociate the band as much as possible from the clichés surrounding live recordings while at the same time allowing audiences to tentatively sample their stage performances. Years later, Missing Link released a live album taken from a concert the band played at the Astor Theatre in Melbourne on 15 January 1982, entitled 'It's still living', without the band's authorisation. Although the album manages to give the listener a fair impression of what a Birthday Party concert sounded like live at that time, the band had never planned to release the material. Keith Glass, who constantly argued that he had invested a lot of money in them and was therefore justified in releasing the band's material as he saw fit, was the initiator behind the album. This and other similar incidents were the main cause of the band's falling out with Glass. Only in 1999 did Rowland and Mick, who had in the meantime obtained the rights to the Birthday Party's back catalogue, decide to release the one and only official live Birthday Party album to date, 'Live 1981-82'. It contains the rest of the material recorded at the Venue gig, as well as material the band had recorded at the Aladdin Club in Bremen, Germany and in Athens, Greece.

But in the spring of 1982, the band was pouring over things much closer to their hearts than releasing live albums. While the band had been working on 'Junkyard' during their stay in Australia, there had been numerous arguments over whether it was time to call it a day, as the band members had come to the conclusion that they had now reached their peak. The arguments continued after the band's return to London and although their shared sense of humour and common language managed to hold things together, there was more than enough tension which would have justified a split at that time. Anyway, The Birthday Party hadn't made any of them rich thus far. Unlike elsewhere in the world, bands on tour in England didn't – and still don't – get paid much for their bother, and often end up shelling out for their bed and board out of their own pockets. Less famous artists have very little say on how their performances should be staged and usually have to rely on the goodwill of their record companies for financial support. Record companies, on the other hand, regard concerts as a form of live advertising and only put their hands in their pockets if the band or individual artist plays along by agreeing to becoming a marketable product, and only then will rewards be forthcoming. The Birthday Party, of course, would never have consented to that kind of sell-out. The band hadn't yet reached the top, and was still a relatively minor portrait in the Hall of Fame, even after the release of 'Junkyard' in July 1982. Keith Glass had yet to hand over any revenue from royalties which he felt justified in withholding to pay for the damage the band had caused in the Melbourne studio, but Nick and the other members of the band suspected that they were being taken for a ride.

When it came down to basics, the band still didn't have much money. Although they had made quite a name for themselves, it didn't look like things were going to change in the near future. The Birthday Party had been adamant in facing off the big record companies in favour of their artistic vision, upholding their view of how a glamorous but totally unpredictable rock band should behave. A lighter, more marketable version still had to be invented. There was no question of The Birthday Party altering its stance now, thus knocking any chance of moving to a multinational record company on the head. However, Nick Cave and Mick Harvey were beginning to suspect that this stubbornness, this anarchistic fuck-you attitude, might just be leading them up a one-way street. The situation was as screwed up as it was absurd. Here was a bunch of existentialists with unsoiled credentials who suddenly found themselves in the midst of a situation with no apparent way out. Something had to be done, but there appeared to be little choice: either split up after having conquered the world or go home, admit defeat and settle down in a place they had striven for so long to leave. Or could The Birthday Party create something new out of their unique blend of blues and punk, something no one had ever heard before? As chance would have it, it was the business-as-usual routine of a band releasing an album and then going on a promotion tour that saved the day.

A month after 'Junkyard' was released, on 3rd June 1982, the band set off for mainland Europe on a tour entitled 'This is the last day of the rest of your life' which kicked off in Eindhoven in the Netherlands. Unbeknown to the band, this tour was to hold more than a few simple twists of fate in store. Four days after the tour kicked off, Nick Cave saw a Die Einstürzenden Neubauten concert on Dutch TV in his hotel room in The Hague. He recognised something of himself in the band's lead singer, Blixa Bargeld, who had a similar egocentric air about him. At the beginning of the 80s, Die Einstürzenden Neubauten had created a new intense and dissonant sound, the beginnings of a German post punk movement that soon came to be known as Neue Deutsche Welle. The Germans even used dead animals to create

sound effects and these, alongside their home-made steel drums, fused with the twisted distortions they played on barely recognisable instruments. Bargeld made an immediate impression on Nick Cave who, in his book 'King Ink', later described Die Einstürzenden Neubauten's lead singer as being '... the most beautiful man in the world. He stood there in a black leotard and black rubber pants, black rubber boots. Around his neck hung a thoroughly fucked guitar. His skin cleared to his bones, his skull was an utter disaster, scabbed and hacked, and his eyes bulged out of their orbits like a blind man's. And yet, the eyes stared at us as if to herald some divine visitation. Here stood a man on the threshold of greatness; here stood a Napoleon victorious amongst his spoils, a conquering Caesar parading his troops, a Christ akimbo on Calvary. (His name was) Blixa Bargeld.' There was a two-week break between The Birthday Party's gigs in Paris and West Berlin. Cave was staying at a hotel in Paris with Anita for a few days, and then followed the rest of the band to Berlin. Nick joined them to record a couple of songs written by Lydia Lunch. She thrived on creating new projects, theatre, art or music, and had just been signed up by the Berlin record label People's Records. She had been working on her 'Honeymoon in Red' project and invited Rowland, his girlfriend Genevieve, Mick, Tracy, and Nick to back her on the album. Unfortunately, things didn't go quite according to plan.

Nobody was really happy with the fruit of their labours. The members of the Birthday Party separated friendship from business and refused to let their name be used to promote a Lydia Lunch album. Then the studio declined to hand out the master cut as there were a number of outstanding bills linked to the project. The ensuing domino effect brought about the collapse of some of the most innovative small independent labels and distributors that had been at the forefront of post punk music in Germany. Rip Off Records, one of the most admired labels of the period but suffering from a lack of secure funding had unwisely invested a considerable amount in People's Records to finance Lunch's 'Honeymoon in Red' project, only to go to the wall. However, the events unfolding during this Berlin intermezzo hadn't come to an end yet. Lunch and Rowland S. Howard had started putting on fifteen-minute one-off performances prior to the shows in Holland and Paris. In Germany, The Birthday Party was also to be supported by Die Haut from Berlin, who had taken their name from Curzio Malaparte's existentialist novel, 'La Pelle – The Skin'. The members of Die Haut, Martin Peter and Remo Park on guitar, the band's Swiss drummer, Thomas Wydler, and Christoph Dreher on bass, got on with the Australians like a house on fire, although they were initially flummoxed by their

dress sense. The Berliners were acutely conscious of their personal appearance and dressed in tight dark suits, Italian shirts and expensive shoes, more fulfilling the cliché of a bunch of Mafia hitmen than a rock band. The members of The Birthday Party couldn't have looked more different, completely casual in their T-shirts, jeans, cowboy boots and horseshoe buckle belts, and, of course, Tracy's Stetson. They had stopped wearing second hand suits years ago.

The members of Die Haut were fond of drinking and relished taking speed. They very nearly hurtled through life with the same alacrity as The Birthday Party, whose members had developed a liking for amphetamines during the tour. To be thrown together with other non-conformists who thought along similar lines, to communicate with musicians who took to the stage not out of some career-driven motive like they did in England, but for whom music was the be all and end all of an anarchistic way of life, was a new experience for the Australians. And Cave was both enthralled and relieved at being on tour with a purely instrumental band. The atmosphere was amiable and their shared passion for music turned the tour into a learning process for all involved. Die Haut, like Die Einstürzenden Neubauten, saw themselves as part of a new generation of German rock bands, even though they were untypical in many ways. They had their roots in the dramatic, histrionic film world of Ennio Morricone but shared a partiality for the wild rock of The Stooges with The Birthday Party, which appealed to them all much more than bland, superficial avant-garde dadaist concepts. *'We were pleasantly surprised when we realised that we could talk to the four from The Birthday Party about everything, films, art and music,'* Christoph Dreher recalls. The feeling was mutual.

Nick Cave and the rest of the band were pleased to have met their new German friends and were fascinated by the stories they had to tell about Berlin and Die Einstürzenden Neubauten, especially Blixa Bargeld. Equally fascinating were their tales of Berlin's nightlife with its self-professed neo-Bohemian ambience, the drugs, and the unique flair that could only be found in a city surrounded by an immense concrete wall. The Birthday Party's last European concert was on 4 July 1982 in Frankfurt after which they returned to London, totally energised by their experiences on the Continent. They had also arranged to meet up with Die Haut at some point in the English capital to record some new material with them. The Germans then flew out to London that July and recorded 'Der karibische Western' and 'Die faulen Hunde von Tijuana' with Lydia Lunch and Nick Cave, tracks that greatly assisted Die Haut in making a name for themselves throughout Germany and beyond. July also saw Nick

Cave inform NME that 'Junkyard', The Birthday Party's second album, would also be their last. That hit the mark. Now there were rumours that The Birthday Party were facing a split – only one fifth of which was true.

July 1982 was a month of difficult decisions for The Birthday Party. Mick, Tracy, Nick and Rowland decided to move to Berlin, as the two weeks they had spent there working – and playing – had been, as Mick Harvey recounts, much more enjoyable than the whole of the two-year period they had spent in London. Phill, however, one of the band's founding members and a friend of Nick's since childhood, was informed that he needn't bother joining them. The rift between them was much too wide and had been erupting into acrimony. It would have been untenable for the band to carry this extra baggage with them to Berlin. Phill had been unable to come to terms with Mick Harvey's musical concepts and was finding it increasingly difficult to fit in. Phill also had a completely different view of life from the rest of the group. Whereas the others were able to agree that they should live life with a proper sense of anarchy and impudence, despite the inner tension and frequent rows, Phill had hoped that they would come to their senses and realise that the band could be the making of their careers. What he failed to perceive was that the band was a microcosm, a patchwork, irrational at its core and not just something that could be transformed into something it wasn't at the drop of a hat. So, Phill was presented with a fait accompli and thrown out of the band. He wasn't left high and dry by any accounts and later became the drummer in the legendary new wave band, The Psychedelic Furs. The Birthday Party, meanwhile, played a farewell concert at The Venue in London on 5 August 1982. With Mick Harvey as their new drummer, the lot of them then headed off for Berlin.

If you were doing a Kid Creole biography I could give you a much better quote – because August Darnell is the opposite of Nick Cave!

Arto Lindsay *(1999)*

Berlin

Have a drink, Malaparte

Curzio Malaparte, „The Skin"

In 1982, the Cold War was still in full swing and the once proud city of Berlin was split into two distinctly separate entities. The Eastern half constituted the capital of the German Democratic Republic, while West Berlin, surrounded on all sides by its communist neighbour, was under the rule of the Allies, the UK, the USA and France. It wasn't until 1990 that both parts of Berlin, at last reunited, officially became part of the Federal Republic. West Berlin was in essence a tiny capitalist island, a thorn in the side of the regime it so openly incensed, and visitors had to either fly into the city, which, in the 1980s, didn't come cheap, or undertake long expeditions through the GDR by car or by train on one of the three transit routes. Traffic jams were commonplace, trains suddenly stopped in mid-journey for no apparent reason, and passport controls were extremely thorough. This made travelling to and from Berlin a laborious task. But it was also a titillating experience to cross this most fortified of European frontiers, to see the Wall first-hand. There were minefields, and the watchtowers along the border were manned by austere-faced officers of the East German army, who indeed were a daunting sight. Visitors to the city left with the impression that they had been somewhere unlike any other European cities, East or West, a place where, no matter where a road or a path led them, they invariably ended up staring at a 7 foot high concrete wall, their journey at an involuntary end. West Berlin's isolated status also meant that there was little heavy industry and its inhabitants had little choice but to make the most of living in a remote environment many outsiders believed was somehow wanting. Things did look worse than they actually were. West Berliners could apply for permits to visit the East. And there were a number of advantages for those who chose to live and work in this bulwark of the capitalist world. State subsidies guaranteed that the standard of living was more or less on a par with that of Western Europe, and over the years billions were invested in West Berlin's infrastructure as the Western Powers could hardly afford to give up this tactical base deep within the Warsaw Pact without abandoning its citizens to an uncertain future. Money was spent on a vast plethora of cultural projects in this strangest of cities which, when it came down to it, was an out-and-out human zoo. There were dozens of theatres and cinemas, countless rock and culture festivals, all of which could never have existed under normal market conditions. West Berlin found strength in celebrating itself like no other city could and was proud of its reputation as an artistic sanctuary, even if, in reality, it could be quite parochial at times.

The city's bizarre situation attracted young West Germans like a magnet. The cost of living was relatively low and Allied Rule meant that West German forces were prohibited from setting foot in the place. Thus, any young man wishing to avoid conscription only had to move to West Berlin and was free of the burden of compulsory military service, an imposition that for many conjured up memories of a chilling militarist past. The main disadvantage of leaving the Federal Republic, however, was that conscientious objectors weren't able to return home to live or work until they had reached the age of thirty or else run the risk of being called up, a nuisance that often resulted in missed career opportunities and a deeply-felt perception of being trapped behind the Berlin Wall forever. The young men and women who had given birth to the city's notorious underground scene regarded West Berlin in the Eighties as a place they could live their lives much as they saw fit. They were part of an anti-bourgeois counter-culture that spouted slogans such as 'whatever it is – legalise it'. There was a festival at the Tempodrom in 1980, an event the future founder of the Love Parade, Dr Motte, still into punk back then, attended alongside Die Einstürzenden Neubauten and the legendary Die Tödliche Doris (Deadly Doris). The festival was the crowning glory of a neo-existentialist-inspired punk movement which had had ramifications throughout Germany. The country's youth, no longer fearful of confronting the dark past their parents had kept the lid on for so long, had suddenly created its own particular brand of punk revolution, admittedly a few years later than elsewhere. The impact it had on society had absolutely nothing in common with the short-lived rebellion England's youth had just about given up on. There, punk had been redefined as a mere fashion statement, unscrupulous manipulators having

espied in it an easy way to make money, stifling the movement in its tracks. The German way was much more intricate, more astute than that. The Berlin underground scene understood punk as a means of facing up to the barbarity of Germany's Nazi past and was no longer afraid to confront politicians on this issue. There was a sudden change of paradigm; people even began saluting each other, their arms outstretched, with ironic 'Sieg Heils!'. They showed their contempt of authority by wearing military outfits or sporting the severe inmate hair-cut of the Concentration Camp victims, for instance. And, of course, there was the music. There was a buzz in the air, at last people were able to communicate a moral decency and sense of shame for what had happened all those years ago. In 1982, this crowd, along with its music, movies, clubs and general outlook, conjured up a new form of artistic perception, at once destructive and foreboding. It had an inherent the-end-is-nigh significance, exemplified in the song 'Kalte Sterne' ('Cold Stars') as Blixa Bargeld knowingly intones: 'Once we're gone, there'll be nothing but the void'. Die Einstürzenden Neubauten were at the forefront of the German scene in 1982 and saw themselves as involved in a face-off with the state and the mental stagnation of its people. Bands like Die Tödliche Doris, Die Haut, Malaria!, Mania D., Borsigwerke, Sprung aus den Wolken and Liaisons Dangereuses all worked and lived in Berlin at this point. Believing themselves to be an avantgarde circle of existentialist performers, they regularly played gigs at the top clubs in town and met up in SO 36, Risiko and Dschungel whenever they were in the mood for a drink. And they could afford to live extravagantly – money went much further in West Berlin than in London or New York.

West Berlin's population had been decreasing for three decades as the city had no real perspective to offer anybody. Whole streets, innumerable shops, and factories stood empty and were waiting for a new lease of life. Not surprisingly, they were frequently taken over by squatters who had established their own set of guidelines, well outside the rule of law. Others, less interested in political radicalism, could legally afford to rent whole floors in factory lofts at prices which seem incredible today. Granted, they didn't have many mod cons but then again there weren't any neighbours around to get on their nerves either. They could turn up their stereos full blast, and bands could even rehearse in their own living rooms without disturbing the neighbours. The nocturnal goings on of those involved in the scene were dictated by amphetamines. It was a common tenet that by staying awake for several days and nights at a time, artists could boost their creative talents, and speed and heroin, mixed with copious amounts of alcohol, were the toast of the day. Strangely enough, one of the great ironies of history, befitting of the rawness of the Berlin scene, was that Nazi bomber pilots were fed amphetamines during the War to keep them alert and to make them more ferocious when facing the enemy, a tradition that no-one minded upholding in those wild, hazy days of 1982.

In August, shortly before Nick Cave's 26th birthday, The Birthday Party arrived in West Berlin and moved into the loft apartment Christoph Dreher shared with the film-maker Heiner Mühlenbrock in Kreuzberg. The Wall virtually ran along the middle of the road and the area couldn't have been more different from the London environment the band was used to. Kreuzberg was much more congenial, less neurotic and nowhere near as hideously expensive as the English capital. The Birthday Party, especially its lead singer Nick Cave, was famous in Berlin, too, and people knew their faces like the back of their hands but knew how to keep their distance unlike in London. This time, the Australians already knew a few people when they arrived, unlike in those desolate first months in England, and they were lucky to be part of a private circle from the outset. They had met Gudrun Gut, lead singer with the group Malaria! and Beate Bartel from Liaisons Dangereuses while on tour in Washington and London. Bartel recalls: *'Berlin was a new experience for them. They didn't need any special permits to travel to the East as they had Australian passports, so they often went on spending sprees in Intershops, stocking up on duty-free vodka and cigarettes.'* For Nick Cave, it was a fortunate turn of events that had led him to a city where he could free himself of many of the constraints of his past life. In addition, West Berlin was a city where people were much more easy-going and unpretentious; they simply took The Birthday Party as it came. The scene was teeming with artists, film-makers, musicians and actors, but the fact that The Birthday Party was famous didn't make any difference to the way they were treated, whereas in hype-mad London, musicians usually saw each other as competition and fans were on the constant lookout for autographs. Like David Bowie, Lou Reed, and Iggy Pop before them, The Birthday Party and Nick Cave learned to appreciate that life in West Berlin was rather unceremonious and that they could maintain some degree of anonymity there, a bit like in New York, a place many musicians from Berlin knew well. The language barrier, too, was another tool to keep the world at arm's length.

In the meantime, the artist Martin Kippenberger had taken over the West Berlin nightspot, SO 36, named after the pre-war postal code for Kreuzberg, and for a while it became the hub of the 'Junge Wilde' art movement and, of course, the punk rock music scene. Exhibitions there opened with live performances which, in themselves, were steeped in artistic idiom. West Berlin was where it was all happening. The gigs Die Ein-stürzenden Neubauten played under the motorway bridges in Schöneberg have become the stuff of legend, as it defied convention with a raucous attitude that could only be found in West Berlin. It was an anarchistic, random act that demanded answers to the central question of whether the time had come to establish a new set of rules. Whereas the London scene had become a banal tourist attraction, in Berlin tourists were kept at bay. The bouncers at SO 36 fed their bloodhounds on raw meat and were fastidious about who they let in to the club. Consequently, the West Berlin music scene, which had welcomed The Birthday Party with open arms right after their arrival in the city, generally reeked of more than just a hint of arrogance. It soon became obvious that, in Berlin, the band wouldn't be forced to play at being the entertainers they would have had to become in London simply in order to survive.

The loft in Dresdner Strasse was a place to set up camp and soon grew into the focal point of The Birthday Party's stay in the city. Dreher recalls: *'They crashed at my place, the door was never locked, and because we were all on speed, we were sure the sun shone out of our asses. When exhaustion set in after a few days of being on our feet, we'd all fall into a deathly coma and sleep it off'*. Nick and the rest of the band were able to relax, to feel at home, for the first time since they had left Australia. There was nothing to get in the way of their creativity and they were rather enjoying being productive. The Birthday Party went on to record two songs they had especially conceived for Anita Lane, 'The Fullness of His Coming' and 'I killed it with a Shoe'. These songs are remarkable, not only because they were the first ones to be released in cahoots with Anita, but also because they go to show just how creative the band had become through their move to West Berlin. On their return from an open-air concert in Athens they had played on 17 September alongside The Fall and New Order, busily setting the scene for the emergence of a Greek post punk scene, The Birthday Party, in its new four-man incarnation, went into Berlin's Hansa-Studio, a former Nazi ballroom, a stone's throw away from the Wall, where David Bowie and Iggy Pop had also recorded some material during their Berlin exile. The Birthday Party laid down four tracks that were more concentrated, compact and structured than any of their previous work, as if the respect they had been greeted with in West Berlin had suddenly unleashed new energies. The four tracks, 'Sonny's Burning', 'Wild World', 'Fears of Gun' and 'Deep in the Woods', released on 'The Bad Seed' EP, are the product of a newly discovered self-confidence which emancipated the band from the influences of their one-time idols. Mick Harvey and Tony Cohen, the band's long-time producer, knew how to use the studio to its best technical advantage and were thus able to refine the band's sound and make it keener. The songs

For a whore is a ditch; and a

strange woman is a narrow pit.

Her house is the way to hell,

going down to the chambers of

death.

are also an excellent example of Cave's obsessive desire to reach out to people with his lyrics. 'In Deep in the Woods', Cave sings from the viewpoint of a murderer who has stabbed a girl to death, deep in the woods as the title says, and, kneeling over her rotting corpse, recalls the event, full of passion. *'This knife feels like a knife, feels like a knife that feels like it's fed.'* Six months previously, Nick Cave's lyrics had been abstractly cryptic and had dealt mainly with his experiments with hard drugs. 'Deep in the Woods' is witness to unimaginable horrors, tightly packaged within the language of poetry: *'The sidewalks are full of love's lonely children, the sidewalk regrets that we had to kill them.'* Even the trees nod silently in agreement as the psychopath throws a last glance heavenward. The stately, heavy blues of The Birthday Party heightens the oppressive atmosphere Nick Cave creates in the deep-rooted scenarios of his songs. Whereas 'Wild World' is a musical illustration of sexual ecstasy, 'Fears of Gun' depicts the brutal loneliness of its protagonist, Gun, after his wife has left him in a heated drunken argument. *'Transistor radio plays an overwhelmingly sad and lonely song, saying oh where she gone? Where she gone? The fears of Gun are the fears of everyone.'* Nick Cave describes the scenes of these songs much more unequivocally, in greater detail than in his earlier work. Gun, for example, just happens to look at the clock and glimpses the strange movement of its hands. When the contours of the room the argument took place in suddenly gain focus in the chairs and tables that have been tipped over, Cave's clarity of perception is intense. All the while, Mick's percussion is verbose and ominous and endorses Nick's fluid diction while heightening the impact of the stories he sings. Rowland and Tracy work in harmony to enrich the tracks with the openness of their style and perfectly round off the atmosphere Mick creates. It had only taken The Birthday Party two months after their flight from London to free themselves from their self-imposed paralysis. Things were starting to come together.

However, it wasn't all just work and no play. The Birthday Party and their girlfriends thought it excellent that pubs and bars never seemed to close in West Berlin. Speed soon helped them forget the familiar London routine where nights tended to end just after midnight. The Risiko Bar became the band's main hang-out, a place for them to either talk or just to collect their thoughts in silence, the consolidation of their private and public lives. Bouncers watched out that only the right kind of punters were allowed in. Risiko only had a bar and a couple of unspectacularly decorated seating areas – and two backrooms anybody had access to. The music was loud, oscillating between Hank William's country and western sounds and the ear-splitting cacophonies of local bands. Alcohol was cheap and regulars didn't think twice about taking drugs

openly, something that gave the place a touch-above-the-rest kind of flair. Nick, Anita, Tracy, Mick, Rowland and the rest of their Australian entourage had become regulars and have never forgotten the endless stream of alcohol that flowed in Risiko. In the right mood, spontaneous concerts or performances by Die Einstürzenden Neubauten would suddenly brighten things up, improvisation at decibel levels that practically raised the roof. Exclusive happenings like these strengthened the familiarity of the Risiko Bar, always jam-packed, and allowed for a peaceful coexistence between punters and the stars who habitually stole the show: usually Nick Cave and Blixa Bargeld. Speed gave them the energy to turn night into day and they often staggered out of Risiko or the Dschungel at six or seven in the morning to either set to work or to spend the day at home in a hyperactive stupor. Many of their friends, totally exhausted, only had one wish – to fall into their beds and drift off into the welcome arms of sleep.

Despite the temptations of West Berlin's nightlife, The Birthday Party could hardly wait to present their material of late and newly-found identity to their fans, so in October and November 1982 the band set off for the UK and Holland to play a series of three gigs in each of those countries. In December of the same year, Nick Cave and Anita Lane visited the group Die Haut in Aachen, a city situated on the border to Belgium and Holland, to record some material with them. Die Haut were working on their second album, 'Burning the Ice', and Nick readily accepted when they asked him to write four songs and do the vocals for them. Three of these, 'Sto-A-Way', 'Pleasure is the Boss', and 'Truck Love' had undertones of the comic-like hermetic cut-ups Cave had penned for the 'Junkyard' album and were more reminiscent of his former style, albeit with a touch of charm, than the new narrative heights he and the band had recently ascended to with 'The Bad Seed' EP. 'Pleasure is the Boss' reduces the world to a humorous playground: *'I am the happiest slave alive around here because pleasure is the boss'*, while 'Dumb Europe', the fourth and final track Cave composed for the album, is more classic drinking air: *'Witness my trail of destruction, trying to leave my drinking place, my feet are magnetised for furniture, the floor's attached to my face'*. Nick, helped along by Anita, had penned the songs on the tour bus after their gigs, or during all night sessions in hotel rooms. To this day, the material recorded with Die Haut, to the great regret of fans, hasn't been made available to a broad public, as the record company, Paradox, went broke just before the finished album was due to be released. But bootlegs of 'Burning the Ice' do bear witness to Die Haut's reputation as a band of the extreme. Due to a technical error during re-mixing, the treble on the record was far too high, leading to the album's sound

being misconstrued as an expression of the raucous tone prevalent in West Berlin at the time, something many other bands then attempted to emulate.

Around about the same time, Nick Cave started incorporating more and more biblical language and imagery into his work. The Bible, with its bloodthirsty tales of fratricide, betrayal, and jealousy as well as its glad tidings of benevolence and love, was a source of unlimited inspiration for him, as was the linguistic beauty of its verses. Cave discovered a proclivity for the psalms and started to express himself in a similar vein to the poetic prose of the King James Bible. Just like in London, he would come to from a night out on speed with fragments of text in his pockets scribbled on scraps of paper but now they recounted tales with overtly Biblical aspects which he could then turn into song. The Bible was both a source of learning for his writing technique as well as a fountain of inspiration, enabling him to pen material that adroitly followed the literary style of Dostoevski, Jim Thompson and Henry Jack Abbott. Basic literary themes such as guilt and absolution, the quest for happiness and the meaning of life itself, not forgetting the thin line between love and hate, turn up again and again in the songs Cave penned from then on. The downside was, now that he had the opportunity to turn his full attention to song-writing and therefore to undertake a voyage of discovery into what his very existence stood for, it had the side-effect of upsetting the equilibrium within the band. Whether the band could compete with the promises of a better life literature is strewn with, was contentious at best. Especially as The Birthday Party was viewed by their fans as a welcome excuse for causing havoc, but, at the same time, seldom as a source of mentally aggressive energy and intellectual wisdom. There didn't seem to be any answer, as there were numerous other, more pressing issues to be confronted. Nick and Rowland had started backbiting each other during the band's tour of Holland in January 1983, and again in England in February. It now seemed that the end of the line was nigh. Tracy, unobtrusive as he was, revelled in mimicking the archetypal rural Australian cowboy and was the only member of the band still comfortable with his life as a Birthday Party rock star. He did not mind the band's constantly changing styles and believed that The Birthday Party hadn't run out of steam yet. But the tension escalated after the band's two-week American tour once they had returned to West Berlin to record their next EP, this one entitled 'Mutiny'.

Even though things appeared to be running smoothly, on the surface at any rate, the situation was becoming untenable. Chris Carr, an old friend of the band who was also their agent in England, had just procured them a recording contract with Mute Records in London. The head of the company, Daniel Miller, meanwhile, had earned enough money with Depeche Mode to be in a better position to sign up The Birthday Party than he had been when he had first met them. The band had just released the 'Bad Seed' EP which had received great critical acclaim. Notwithstanding, the giant swastika on the cover, a bleak expression of what was perfectly acceptable in underground West Berlin, caused such a rumpus in England that the band was catapulted into the centre of a flaming media controversy. But more intense were the internal disputes as to what musical direction the band should be taking. Whereas Rowland wanted to continue as before, Nick was beginning to see his musical perspective in a new light, a format that gave him a lot more scope. He was a great fan of the music of Bob Dylan, Elvis, and Leonard Cohen, but any rapprochement with this type of music was simply just not on in a band like The Birthday Party.

The director Heiner Mühlenbrock, one of the Germans the band stayed with when they were in the city, used to listen to them playing in the apartment and he hit upon the idea of filming the 'Mutiny' sessions. He produced a 25-minute take which was never to be officially released, a video that documents the end of the band as they record the blues ballad 'Jennifer's Veil' at the Hansa-Studio. Filmed in broad daylight, the camera captures images of the wooden floor, shows the instruments and mikes being set up, and catches the mood of four taciturn musicians, none of whom really had anything much to say to each other. Rowland S. Howard's melancholic guitar chords carry the song and are monument to his turning a vague snippet of a melody into a complete work. The camera records for posterity the band's endeavours at arranging the track, hardly a word spoken. When anybody speaks, any constructive form of cooperation is smothered by loud bickering. Rowland and Nick are seen to shrug off all responsibility and let Mick sort things out. Only Tracy doesn't seem to be affected by the negative tension in the room. Understandably, Mick would later describe the film as 'depressive'. Mühlenbrock's court mètrage is a riveting document thanks to its excellent cutting technique and deliberate lack of commentary. It expertly illustrates the decline and fall of one of the most physical rock bands of the era, while depicting the music in its rawest of forms. The band didn't manage to finish the EP, as they were scheduled to set off on a tour of Australia and New Zealand. Easier said than done. Mick put his foot down and solidly refused to go. He had often indicated that he wouldn't be going along, as earning Australian $80,000 didn't seem worth it, but Nick, Rowland and Tracy hadn't really taken him at his word. For them $80,000 was a lot of money, so they kept on narking Mick to come along until he finally blew his top.

On top of all that, bands usually only take a tiny amount of the money they earn from touring home with them, most of it spent on unforeseen expenses, excessive shopping sprees, and drugs. Moreover, Mick no longer felt any strong desire to go on tour with a band that was constantly rowing. Chris Carr had even proposed going on a year-long world tour to earn enough money to keep them afloat for a while. *'We would have spent a whole year getting on each other's nerves,'* Mick recalls, *'and that would certainly have thrown us off track.'* So, Mick and Katy declined the offer of a flight ticket to Melbourne and The Birthday Party played its final gig with Mick in the line-up at the Electric Ballroom in Camden, London. The remaining three members of the band found themselves under enormous pressure as a result of Mick's departure. They would have to find a new drummer in Australia, someone they could implicitly trust with their material, and they sensed that the Australian tour would most probably be The Birthday Party's last. The band finally roped in Des Hefner, who played percussion in The Marching Girls, for the 11 gigs they had scheduled in Australia and the five in New Zealand. Hefner soon grasped that there was no way he could follow in Mick Harvey's footsteps and the band's performances weren't up to their usual standard as they hadn't had enough time to rehearse. The Birthday Party, in this new line-up, played full houses and acted like true rock stars on and off the stage. However, the band was somehow bereft and could only play slow ballads and grooves, Hefner not having had the time to sink his teeth into anything else. Nick, Rowland and Tracy would have preferred not to have done the tour at all and the difficulties Mick's leaving them in the lurch had caused still had to be resolved. 18 days after their final Australian gig, at the Venue Club in Melbourne, on 9 June, an embarrassed band played a second farewell concert, this time at the Seaview Ballroom. Out of the $80,000 originally promised, each of the band members received a measly $1,000 for their efforts – the tour managers had managed to blow the lot on unnecessary extravagance. This wasn't enough to pay for the flight back to London where the musicians had planned to remix the 'Mutiny' EP with Mick that August. Continent-hopping didn't come cheap in the 80s.

The constant flare-ups, the rut they had fallen into, and their wont for acting it up during the farewell tour took their toll on the band, both physically and mentally. Drained, worn out, and suspecting that they had all made a huge mistake, Nick and Rowland turned to their families for solace. During these weeks of peace and quiet after a disastrous tour, the musicians finally came to understand that they had just buried the fruits of ten year's hard labour. Once the 'Mutiny' EP was finished, The Birthday Party would cease to exist. Mute Records, in full agreement with the band, released a press statement to announce the news: *'In view of the events of this year, it has become obvious that new challenges are needed to sustain our creative vitality. Rather than continue regardless of a better judgement (i.e., for money or through lack of daring) and diminishing the impact of a rock, it has been decided to end The Birthday Party. Individual plans are not definite but we hope this decision will be productive as it its intent.'* It is all the more astonishing that the 'Mutiny' EP leaves the listener with an impression of an intact, thoroughly vigorous band. Three of the four tracks on the EP, 'Swampland', 'Jennifer's Veil', and 'Say a Spell' were recorded with Rowland on guitar, while Blixa Bargeld plays guitar on the fourth. After a mighty argument in the Britannia Row Studios in London in August '83, Rowland disappeared into the night, four days before the final touches were to be put to the EP. Instead of trying to talk him into coming back to finish what he had started, Nick asked Blixa whether he would mind standing in for Rowland at short notice. Luckily for him, Die Einstürzenden Neubauten were in town working on their own album. It was a curious twist of fate that it was Bargeld, only occasionally guitar in Die Einstürzenden Neubauten, who played the final notes on the sinking ship that was The Birthday Party. He was more than eager, however, to play guitar in a band he could respect, as he and Nick had once shared the stage at a party thrown by Beate Bartel in Berlin, something he had thoroughly enjoyed. Nick knew that Bargeld's regressive, distorted style would go down well, in any case, his experimental, extreme sound would appear much more dynamic than Rowland's. Bargeld's technique bowled them over in its intensity, although he was anything but a virtuoso. Yet it was exactly this limitation that instilled the track 'Mutiny in Heaven' with a life of its own; steeped in a repetitive, headstrong monotonous rhythm, it was Bargeld and his guitar that turned the song into an urban blues classic.

'Mutiny in Heaven' was received as a dignified requiem for probably the only true rock band of the early eighties, not just because of Bargeld's excellent guitar work, but also due to Cave's passionately sung vocals. The song is a complex linguistic collage in which Cave exorcises the demons of his drug addiction, comparing the needle marks in the arm of a young girl to infernal torment. The singer in the guise of a raggedy angel, his wings dingy and barely holding together (*'damn things hardly flap'*), sings as he falls from Heaven: *'If this is Heaven ah'm bailing out'.* Cave sings of insurrection in paradise, images of man invading heaven like a plague, and so confronts God with the words: *'Ah git down on ma knees and start to pray'.* 'Mutiny in Heaven' doesn't only make great use of biblical imagery. Cave also took much of the inspiration for the language he used in the song from Flannery O'Connor's novel 'Wise Blood' whose linguistic appeal combines modern colloquialisms with a kind of Shakespearean dialect. His choice of words is archaic and the modified spellings arouse feelings of an exotic, fierce vernacular, to amazing effect. The religious diction allows Cave to identify with the protagonist of the song without necessarily having to identify with its content.

No matter how gruesomely the stories told come over, his literary prowess enables Cave to take on the role of a sinner, a heretic or a psychopath who has committed heinous crimes – he can murder, debauch, and wreak havoc at will. The detachment between the singer and the song is attained through the linguistic psalm-like style he deploys that exudes an aura of infallible truth. But Cave's unexpected outing as a narrator delving into a treasure trove of subtle literary tools with ironic reserve also caused much misunderstanding. The music press accused him of being a misogynist, as women were either victims or downright dominant figures in his songs, creatures who made men's life a living hell. There are three untimely deaths on the 'Mutiny' EP, each one of them tragic. In 'Swampland', the singer, slowly sinking into oblivion in quick-sand (*'Quixanne, ah'm in its grip, sinkin in the mud'*), can hear the rabble coming to lynch him (*'So cum ma executioners! Cum bounty hunters! Cum mah county killers!'*), after he has killed his mistress, a girl called Lucy (*'Lucy, ya made a sinner outta me, now ah'm burnin like a saint'*). Swampland's protagonist was in love with her, and now trapped in a quagmire as he recalls the crime he has committed, is condemned to helplessness till death consumes him. 'Swampland' is the torchsong of a murderer in the last few minutes of his life, unable to move, no choice but to either drown or be stoned to death by the approaching mob. Resplendent with passion and rancour, Cave sings: *'They hunt me like a dog, down in Swaaaaaaaaamp Land'*. In 'Swampland', unmistakably the Mississippi Delta of William Faulkner, the mythical birthplace of the Blues, racial segregation and religious fanatics, Cave reveals the scene of his novel, 'And the Ass Saw the Angel', in which a mute chooses suicide in a swamp after having murdered a girl, recounting the story of his life in an inner monologue. The third victim on the 'Mutiny' EP is, again, a woman. In the stately ballad, 'Jennifer's Veil', an unsuspecting man by the name of Frankie returns to the place he had once left, a town by the sea. The singer warns him: *'Leave on the next train, your Jennifer she just ain't the same.'* Cave implores: *'Get back! Don't reach out! Get back, and get that lantern out of my room!'* The scenario isn't quite as explicit a backdrop as in 'Swampland', this time events taking place in the past, evoked by Frankie's arrival by train, a motif of innumerable blues songs, and the tall ships in the harbour: *'Another ship is ready to sail, the rigging is tight, tight like Jennifer's veil.'* The one thing all three songs have in common is that Cave is now much more

present at the heart of the proceedings, no longer a passive bystander. Profiting greatly from the new role Nick Cave is playing, these tracks realigned the power structures within the band to such a degree that there was no going back to the way things were before. Cave had elevated himself to the position of a medium, someone who understood how the world worked, someone whose words held a message, just like the blues singers' of the early 20th century. Now it was the message that was the focal point of the songs, not the music per se. Never before had the band's musical expression been so collected, so reduced to the essentials, so enticing. But Cave's high-profile performance meant that the band had become secondary, a mere backdrop for the tales of life, love and death only he could portray.

When 'Mutiny' was released, the band confounded all their critics who had regarded them as a bunch of arrogant, egocentric, and depraved junkies (*'The most degenerate, disgusting bunch of drug addicted rock stars, Sodom and Gomorrha, have crept across our border – Brisbane News'*). This was the last time the four of them would work together, all of them unanimous in that this supreme example of how they could pool their talents if they set their minds to it would be their last. Cave had actually suggested renaming the band 'The Bad Seeds' when they had finished the EP of the same name in West Berlin. He felt it could have given impetus to the new musical and narrative styles the band had unleashed on the world after Phill Calvert's departure. The others weren't too keen on the idea, as agreeing would have degraded them to the position of mere musical accompaniment for their lead singer. The Birthday Party was much more than that, a group that wasn't organised with the same kind of pecking order as many other bands. Quite the contrary, The Birthday Party lived off the equality of its members and their differing musical concepts. It was this democratic structure that finally hammered the last nail into the coffin; the music might have profited from the constant rowing, but the social cohesion of the band had suffered greatly as a result. If they had buried the hatchet earlier on, they might have been able to come to some agreement on how decisions were to be taken, thus avoiding the imminent split. They could have elected Cave as the leader of the band and elevated Mick Harvey to the position of main arranger, for example, but the breakdown in communication steadfastly prevented any form of open discourse. The bell had rung time on The Birthday Party. Nick Cave spent the summer of 1983 in London.

Melville, Faulkner, Milton, Twain, Dylan, Cave. He continues to amaze. How he's kept his sense of humor through the last 20 years I'll never understand.

Henry Rollins *(1999)*

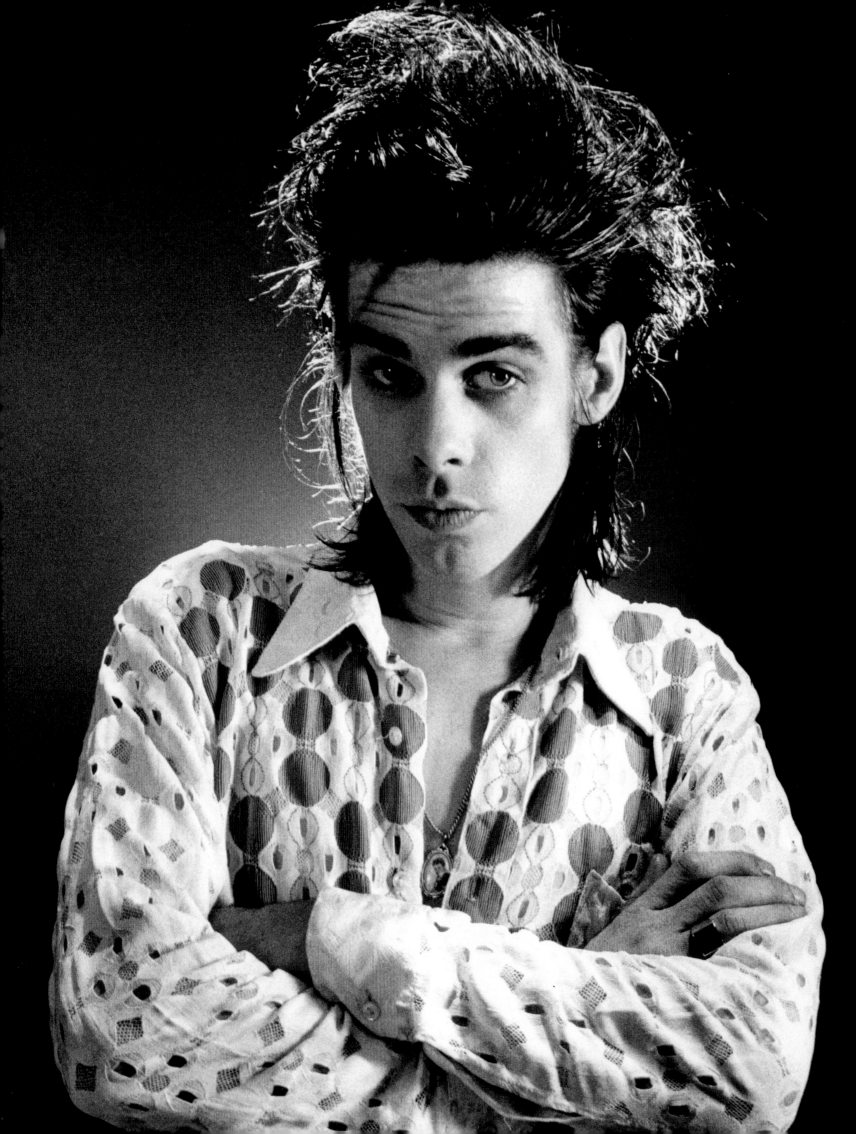

Blues

Crows aver that just one of their kind would suffice to tear down Heaven. This is certainly true, but it doesn't prove anything – because Heaven signifies: impossibility of crows.

Franz Kafka,
'Observations on Sin, Suffering, Hope and The True Way'

The history of rock also documents the lives of its singers. In the early decades of the 20th century the birth of new recording technologies and the gramophone, especially, meant that people could now listen to music in the comfort of their own homes. Country and blues were very popular then, but music styles change over time, each era producing its own idols whose stars burn brightly in the firmament of rock legend. For instance, the music of Blind Willie McTell, Leadbelly, Robert Johnson, Blind Lemon Jefferson, Hank Williams, Elvis Presley, Tony Bennett, Frank Sinatra, Lee Hazlewood, Johnny Cash, John Lee Hooker, Bob Dylan, and Leonard Cohen, to name but a few, will never be forgotten, but, above all, it is the wondrous qualities of their voices that make them immortal. The same holds true for rock bands. The vocal expression of their lead singers is often much more captivating than the undeniable talents of the groups they front. We feel compelled to take a keen interest in their careers, even long after the groups they were in have split up, because their voices mould our souls and reach into our hearts, thus becoming an indispensible feature of our lives. By the time the members of The Birthday Party went their seperate ways, Nick Cave had already enjoyed some of his biggest successes. Now that the band had been consigned to the annals of history, he had no idea of what the future would bring. So, why not set his sights high and reach for the stars? Free from the constraints of being in a collective, Cave now aspired to becoming a singer of note. Throughout his entire career, he had managed to set himself apart from the norm and had constantly shunned the conventions of the music business. Creating a trademark for himself, becoming a 'celebrity', might have helped to sell records in the shortterm but would have compromised Cave's artistic identity, turning him into a marketable product in the process. Instead, he was resolute in creating an image that showed the world what he was really made of, warts and all. Now that The Birthday Party had ceased to exist, what was Cave to tell his fans? And more importantly, would they listen?

In September 1983, Nick asked Mick Harvey whether he would be willing to work with him on his first solo album as he was conveniently staying in London. Cave had come up with the idea for a new experimental project but wanted to work with musicians he had come to know and trust over the years who would help him create a new blend of music and a new sound. Harvey, intrigued by the project, agreed even though Cave had made it clear from the outset that he would be the one calling the shots. Nick was in a reasonably fortunate position. The Birthday Party had been used to playing full houses, tickets for their concerts had sold like hot cakes wherever they went, and their records had now attained minor cult status. However, Cave's solo career may never have gotten off the ground, as he hadn't quite reached the top yet. Luckily Daniel Miller, the boss of his record company, had faith in him, as did most of his admirers. Miller was certain that fans would stand by Cave as a solo performer with the same ardour and loyalty they had always shown The Birthday Party. Nick himself was eager to put this to the test. Mute gave the go-ahead, booked the Garden Studio in London and invited Blixa Bargeld over from Berlin. He and Nick had worked extremely well together on The Birthday Party's 'Mutiny' EP and the two men had struck up a genuine friendship. Therefore, it seemed only appropriate that Bargeld participate in this ambitious project, even if his expertise on the guitar wasn't quite that of a virtuoso. Bargeld was chuffed at having been asked to work with Cave and saw being in the backing group of an artist he greatly admired as a tremendous artistic and personal challenge. Playing second or even third fiddle to Nick and Harvey posed no problem whatsoever as, being the lead singer, songwriter and image provider in his own group, Die Einstürzenden Neubauten, he already knew full well what it was like to be a star in his own right. He looked forward to working with Cave, and, at the same time, to making a new name for himself on the international stage. The fourth pillar of the band's initial line-up was Jim Thirlwell, still based in London, and better known by his stage names Foetus and Clint Ruin. Before long, the hastily assembled crew started working on

four new tracks written by Cave, 'A Box for Black Paul', 'Saint Huck', 'Wings Off Flies' and an early version of 'From Her to Eternity'.

A common element to all of these songs was their downbeat tempo, which gave much more scope to Cave's vocals. Speed, used as a weapon in their personal *war against sleep*, as Bargeld termed it, was a source of never-ending, waking motivation and enabled them to create moments of absolute musical intensity. It soon became apparent, however, that Thirlwell didn't fit in with the musical concept Cave was trying to forge. Barry Adamson, who, two years previously, had stood in for Tracy Pew while he was serving his prison sentence in Melbourne, was therefore hired to do the job instead. Adamson's contribution helped to consolidate a new style, a sombre, fundamental shuffle between acoustic spirals and arrangements that were heavily influenced by the blues. Work on the album was interrupted in October as Lydia Lunch had arranged three shows for the end of the month in the States, two in New York and one in Washington DC, bang in the middle of the country's Halloween celebrations. So Cave, Lunch and Thirlwell crossed the Atlantic in the illustrious company of Marc Almond who had just left his internationally acclaimed band, Soft Cell, at the peak of their success to pursue a solo career. The four of them, together with the then head of the british Die Einstürzenden Neubauten fan-club Jessamy Calkin, were a close-knit circle back in London and enjoyed spending time in each other's company, despite any musical differences Cave and Thirwell may have had. The American project had been baptised 'The Immaculate Consumptive' and offered a welcome opportunity of not just having a good time, but of earning some money as well.

At the first gig in New York's Danceteria Discotheque, Cave premiered his rendition of the Elvis classic 'In the Ghetto', and 'A Box for Black Paul' arranged as a piano ballad. He was accompanied on 'In the Ghetto' by a backing tape that Barry Adamson, Marc Almond's pianist Annie Hogan, and Blixa Bargeld had recorded for him but had planned to play the piano himself for his rendering of 'A Box for Black Paul'. However, the opening evening in NYC well and truly scuppered his plans. Thirlwell was so electrified by the audience and the dimensions of the stage that he felt a strange compulsion to do an imitation of Jerry Lewis and started stomping around on the piano-keys, wrecking the instrument in the process. The wild bunch thoroughly enjoyed their trip to New York. Lunch and Cave dug into each other during a televised press conference, but this set-to was nothing they couldn't handle and at least gave them something to remember the trip by. It was clear from the outset, though, that the three performances were to be a one-off. Lunch and Thirlwell were pursuing a number of projects while Marc Almond and Nick Cave would be kept busy sorting out their own solo careers, learning to put the past behind them, and preparing for a new future. Instead of continuing with his new album, Nick and Anita went to Los Angeles. It wasn't a visit he would remember fondly. The pair of them had been an item for seven years, but Nick had been far from being the model partner and Anita had finally had her fill of his indiscretions. Fed up with living the life of a Nomad, she wanted to settle down. Cave was due to return to Australia to play a series of gigs at the turn of the year, so while he took a plane to Melbourne, Anita stayed behind in LA with an American journalist she had grown close to. The breakdown of their relationship hit Nick badly, although women were still throwing themselves at his feet. But he was in no mood for them and, suffering from a broken heart, he headed home to the sunny climes of Australia to lick his wounds.

With more than a pinch of self-irony, the Australian tour had been billed as 'Man or Myth?'. The backing band, The Cavemen, no less, had the same line-up as The Birthday Party but without Rowland S. Howard. Mick Harvey was on percussion, Tracy Pew, now studying politics and philosophy in Melbourne, on bass, and Barry Adamson on guitar. To round things off, Nick also roped in Melbourne guitarist Hugo Race, to give the band more of a bluesy kind of feel. Cave would have preferred his friend and colleague Blixa Bargeld to have come along for the ride, but he was too busy with other projects to fit the tour into his tight schedule. Nick Cave and The Cavemen performed some of The Birthday Party's old material, including 'Swampland', 'Jennifer's Veil', and 'Mutiny in Heaven', alongside cover versions of Screamin' Jay Hawkins's 'I Put a Spell on You' and Leonard Cohen's 'Avalanche'. 'Wings Off Flies' and 'Saint Huck', two of the more recent songs Nick had penned in London, were also included in the sets during the tour.

Although tickets for the band's gigs were selling well, Nick was glad to be home for other, more personal reasons. Just like in previous years, visiting Australia at New Year was a welcome opportunity to escape the drab European winter and to tank up on energy. Just what the doctor ordered, as far as Nick was concerned – he was still pining after Anita. They had gone through too much together for the bond between them to be completely severed, but the sudden end to their relationship unleashed a powerful sense of loss in Nick Cave. He hadn't been feeling too great about

himself for a while, anyway, so he tried to take his mind off things by throwing himself into his work. There was some interest in his staging the short one-act plays he had written two years previously with Lydia Lunch. This 'Theatre of Revenge' was an artistic concept that blended established forms of art with a destructive impulse, expressed through pornography and violence, in a show of ultimate confrontation. Lunch and Cave purposely overstepped the mark of accepted theatrical practices in these one-act performances, their stage directions, for example, requiring that the audience be placed around four separate platforms where the plays would be acted out simultaneously. The plays themselves were more a form of literary art than traditional theatre, and Nick had to rework them during his sojourn Down Under so that they could be acted out on a real stage. However, a lack of funding soon put an end to that idea, Melbourne would have to miss out. Nonetheless, in directing his energies into his work, Cave was able to project his frustrations into something worthwhile that, more importantly, took his mind off his personal problems.

Mick Harvey had a number of interests he felt he should pursue while he was at home in Australia. Simon Bonney, who had been trying out various new line-ups for his band, Crime And The City Solution, asked Mick to help him out with a couple of demos for his next album in an attempt at earning international recognition. At that time, Bonney had only really attained celebrity status in Australia and was keen to expand his horizons. Hence, in 1984, Harvey took it upon himself to play a decisive role in two bands at the same time, putting himself under enormous pressure as a result, but steadfastly maintained that his decision had nothing at all to do with Nick's solo career. One by one, Barry Adamson, Hugo Race, Nick Cave, and Mick Harvey returned to London, where they were joined by Blixa Bargeld, to continue working on Nick's album. They cut a number of tracks in London's Trident Studios that would later feature on the A-side of 'From Her to Eternity'. In addition to a new version of the title track Cave had co-written with Anita the last time she had been in London, the band also recorded cover versions of Leonard Cohen's 'Avalanche', Elvis's 'In the Ghetto', as well as three tracks Nick had penned, 'Cabin Fever', 'Well of Misery' and 'The Moon is in the Gutter'. Cave hadn't yet been able to decide whether his backing band was to become a permanent feature, so the only mention they got on the cover of the first single, 'In the Ghetto', and the ensuing album, 'From Her to Eternity', was the innocuous: 'Nick Cave featuring the Bad Seeds'. But it was exactly these 'Bad Seeds' that helped Cave to produce a rock album of monumental proportions. Sufficient incentive for Nick and the members of the band to put their heads together and finally decide to keep the new name.

The songs on 'From Her to Eternity', reduced to their bare essentials, are nothing less than masterpieces. The poetic tragedy of most of the tracks on this, Cave's first solo album, interweave a deeply sensed desolation, and a helpless fury at the wantonness of a world that can never redress the heart-ache of man. In 'Cabin Fever', Cave reveals the pain of his separation from Anita in a haunting tale of a sailor, reminiscent of Melville's Captain Ahab. Out at sea in the middle of winter, the captain sweeps his meagre meal from his cabin table, his arm bearing a tattoo of Christ and the inscription A-N-I-T-A. He scratches the passing of time into the beams of the ship like a convict incarcerated in a desolate cell. *'He tallies up his loneliness notch by notch, for the sea offers nuthin to hold or touch.'* The ship is tossed around by a storm, empty liquor bottles falling like crystal ninepins, making the story appear all that more enchanted. The title track of the album, 'From Her to Eternity', just as fatalistic, is the monologue of a man who, pacing up and down in his apartment, sees in the woman upstairs at number 29 the fulfilment of all his dreams. He can hear her striding, bare-foot, across the floor, her tears leaking through the floorboards, dripping on to his face. *'Hot tears come splashing down, leakin through the cracks, down upon my face, ah catch them in my mouth.'* The man steals pages from her diary, hence becoming party to her nightmares. His desire for the object of his passion, makes him obsessed by the thought of her heart belonging only to him, but knowing that if it ever did, the fires of his longing would wane. *'But ah know that to possess her, is therefore not to desire her, that lil' girl would just have to go! Go! From her to eternity.'* In 'Saint Huck', Cave narrates the story of Huckleberry Finn in a highly-charged comic-like allegory. Born and bred in the country, on the banks of the Big River, Saint Huck follows the call of the big bad city *('O come to me, O come to me! Is what the dirty city say to Huck')*. There he falls victim to corruption of mind and lands in the gutter before eventually winding up dead. Nothing can protect him, not even the innocent song he clings to, its power to ward off evil diminished forever. *'And a bad-bline-nigger at the piano puts a sinister-bloo-lilt to that sing-a-long. Huck senses something's wrong!!'* Soon Saint Huck, having lost his faith in the deliverance only the song can bring, barely whistling it as he progresses towards his destiny, becomes indifferent to his doom. *'See ya Huck. Good luck!'* His fate sealed, Cave sings its finality with poetic licence, *'And the rats and the dogs and the men all come and put a bullet through his eye.'* Neither does the protagonist in 'Well of Misery' fare any better. Leaning over

the brim of a well, a woman's dress floating in the water below him deadening the sound of his tears as they fall, he recounts his story. Then in 'A Box for Black Paul' whose initials could also be read as 'A Box for the Birthday Party', Cave adapts the speech of blues singer John Lee Hooker and weaves his words into a lament. *'Well you know I've been a bad man, And Lord knows I've done some good too, But I confess my soul will never rest, Until you build a box for my girl too.'* The song has often been interpreted as a parting cry to The Birthday Party, but is equally a tender fare-well to his soul-mate and former love of his life, Anita Lane.

There are other tracks on the album that are more capricious, songs that leave far behind the hopeless purgatories Cave's characters usually have to go through. In 'Wings Off Flies', the singer plucks the wings off dead flies, killed as they collide with the windowpane. *'She loves me, she loves me not, she loves me...'* Cave is scoffing at religion and poking fun at his own misanthropic image, his gushing words an affirmation that he has found the key to the gates of paradise, *'You get the solitude and mix it with sanctuary and silence, then bake it!'* As a final gesture, Cave's protagonist demands, not without irony, to be tried by Divine Justice for his hatred of mankind. Cave found much of the inspiration for the album in his memories of Anita and she features on the cover along with Polaroids of the actual band members. Although she doesn't figure anywhere on the album in person, nobody can deny that her spirit is crystallised on 'From Her to Eternity', an album that immortalises Lane as the muse and addressee of many of its lyrics. The album would never have turned out to be a timeless classic if the music hadn't taken on such sharp contours. Cave seduces by forgoing the effects chart bands like The Eurythmics, Wham! and Van Halen had turned into trademarks in 1983. All the songs on 'From Her to Eternity' have obvious blues elements which Cave successfully incorporates within a contemporary context. But it is down to the group of musicians he gathered around him that the gradual tone of the songs manages to blossom into a mood of heady abstraction. Leornard Cohen's 'Avalanche', for example, the album's opening track, has such an austere arrangement that one wrong note would suffice to ruin the whole mood. Bargeld's guitar is blaringly demure, Harvey's percussion reduced to sparse moments of drum rolls, the song resonant with Adamson's bass, perfectly befitting of a love gone sour. Cave's threateningly intoned vocals are grim as he publicly exorcises his relationship with his audience: *'Do not dress in those rags for me / I know you are not poor / And do not love me quite so fiercely now / When you know that you are not sure'*. Cohen later declared that he was greatly impressed by Cave's rendition of his song. The tracks 'From Her to Eternity' and 'Saint Huck' are poignant in their vehemence, strangely reminiscent of The Birthday Party's greatest moments. The album is more accessible, more refined than past recordings, and Cave at last has an opportunity to use his voice to its full potential. In 'Well of Misery', the Bad Seeds form a choir that echoes the lines Cave has just sung in a call-and-response technique akin to that of early blues music, its roots steeped deep in religious incantation. It is no coincidence that this was the style much loved by Negro slaves, the Cotton Pickers of the American Deep South, and 'Well of Misery' reflects its intense, elementary temperament, vacillating gently between obsession and finely-tuned irony.

When, in September 1983, the band had gone into the studio for the first time as a team, they had no indication where this collaboration would lead them or whether the band would become a permanent fixture. 'From Her to Eternity' was intended to be no more than the attempts of a young singer to free himself as best as he could from the jaws of the past by inventing a fresh, original, experimental style. But Cave and the band were amazed by the sound they had been able to entice from their instruments. These four sensitive but intractable men, whose only common tie was their friendship with Nick Cave, had managed to create a finished album that revealed such keen precision, a combined effort that was the result of expertise on all sides.

Nick and the Bad Seeds set off on a European tour scheduled for April and May 1984. It had initially been billed as 'Nick Cave and the Cavemen', but at their first gig the band unanimously decided to throw the name overboard and decided to opt for 'Nick Cave and The Bad Seeds' instead. Nick and The Bad Seeds had every right to be satisfied with the 18 concerts they played in Holland, Germany, and Denmark as well as back in England. As anticipated, many fans were disappointed ('You sold out'), while others positively celebrated the transformation Cave had gone through. They recognised that he had matured, that sentimental ballads like 'A Box for Black Paul' and his encore 'In the Ghetto' were proof that he was capable of expressing unexpected tenderness. Media reaction was even more unambiguous than that of the fans. 'From Her to Eternity' was released while Cave was on tour with the band in May, and critics were feting him as the future hero of blues and rock. For the first time, the music press was united in its judgement and Cave's espousal of the blues was received as signalling his move away from punk. The NME, the UK's top music magazine, summarised 'From Her to Eternity' as *one of the greatest rock albums ever made'.*

However, in 1984, his daily shot of heroin was much more important to Nick than the acclaim critics were now bestowing on him. He had a nasty habit of disappearing to try and score before concerts and sometimes didn't turn up until shortly before the show was about to start, the others nervous that they might have to call the whole thing off. He frequently risked life and limb, especially when deals turned out to be set-ups or when knives were pulled. But much to the surprise of those closest to him, his band of musicians in particular, Cave always managed to perform with impressively precise dedication and passion. Not that his drug addiction made working with him easy, despite all his professionalism and inspiration. Fortunately, one thing that cemented relationships between the band members was the mature manner in which they dealt with the whole drug-taking malarkey, and even though the public eye was mainly on Cave, he certainly wasn't the only one among them who was into mind-enhancing substances. Shortly after the end of the European tour, Nick Cave and The Bad Seeds set off for the USA for a three-week series of ten concerts at venues all over the country. They performed with their usual propensity, of course, their concentration unimpeded, but otherwise they were living on a knife edge. Whenever he had time, Nick buried himself in the book he was writing. Since Evan English had asked him during his last visit to LA whether he would be interested in writing a movie script, Cave had been piecing together fragments of a story. On 22 June 1984, while in Pasadena, California, with The Bad Seeds, Nick met up with English and his friend and colleague Paul Goldman, otherwise known as the Rich Kids, old friends from Australia who were now based in LA. Assisted by John Hillcoat, they managed to shoot the video for Cave's new single, 'In the Ghetto', in just two days. The video doesn't exactly show Cave from his best side. He was drawn and pale and looked like a ghost amidst the cardboard decoration of the set, which was meant to represent a Christian chapel. The clip is a shocking document to the discrepancy between Cave's rousing stage performances and the hours he had to while away between them. 1984 hadn't been a good year. All the same, he accepted the Rich Kids's offer of staying with them in LA as their guest and set to work on the script, free of the media circus and the tribulations that came with touring.

This was a move that paid off, at least for Cave. English, Hillcoat and Goldman locked their friend into a rented bungalow, the fridge packed with junk food and beer. In the evenings, they had him read aloud the passages he had spent the day writing. Cave was descending more and more into the world of his character, Euchrid Eucrow, who had first seen the light of day in his song 'Swampland'. Now he em-

barked on putting to paper the intricate story of his murderous protagonist. In the belief that God has shown him the path to salvation, Eucrow acts without conscience or remorse. Writing the manuscript was laborious, Cave constantly reworking the text and making corrections. Like in any type of serious writing, decisions had to be taken on formal aspects and content. The only problem of note his producer friends could discern was Nick's strict refusal to ensure that his script was technically practicable. Cave was resolute, otherwise much of the manuscript would have to be scrapped. For instance, the sequence that years later would become the prologue to his first novel 'And the Ass Saw the Angel': the scene of a crow circling a small mountain valley and an old-time township in the Deep South would have had to be cut. The producers tried to convince him that it would break their limited budget to film the scene from the air, as would the construction of a 1940s set, but to no avail. The worries raised by Nick's sorties into LA's gangland to buy drugs were trivial in comparison. During the three months Cave spent in exile in LA he got to know a number of other musicians – Henry Rollins, lead singer with the hardcore punk band Black Flag, Jeffrey Lee Pierce, and Kid Congo Powers, the guitarist from The Gun Club, a great band that was receiving much critical acclaim at the time. These chance encounters developed into friendships and, in the case of Kid Congo Powers, a professional relationship was also to transpire. When Nick returned to London at the end of September and then on to West Berlin, he left behind a movie script that nobody could turn into a film – but he did have the draft for his first novel.

In West Berlin, Nick Cave, Blixa Bargeld, Barry Adamson, and Mick Harvey, who had been working with Simon Bonney and Rowland S. Howard on yet another incarnation of Crime And The City Solution, got together for a couple of recording sessions. Hugo Race had founded a new group in Melbourne, The Wreckery, and was too busy back home to take time out and work with Cave in Europe. Nick wrote most of the material for the new album in a matter of weeks, the songs dealing with motifs from the manuscript for his novel. Another European tour scheduled for November, this time taking in Italy, Spain, London, Amsterdam, and Berlin offered The Bad Seeds a good opportunity to try out their new material. Now that they had had enough time to get some work in, the band, reduced to a trio by Hugo Race's defection, went into Berlin's Hansa Studio to record a second album. The Bad Seeds had been a permanent fixture for quite some time now, and the various tours had given the musicians time to get to know each other better. They no longer felt that they had something to prove and their recording sessions profited

greatly from the harmonised sound the band was now capable of producing. Cave's new songs radiated a sense of calm and fellowship, again taking up on the blues music of the thirties and forties but much more blatantly than on the previous album.

'The First Born is Dead', strangely enough, is a classic example of an album that was ripped to shreds by the critics, not because of its intrinsic value, but because they had an axe to grind. The album wasn't meant to be measured as a follow-on from 'From Her to Eternity' by any means, but the critics saw it as a new way of settling old debts. They already knew all about his drug addiction that had been the subject of public debate for years. Not really aware of what he was doing and foolishly trusting the media hacks around him, Cave had granted quite a few journalists insights into his private life that many knew how to exploit, while others simply basked in the glory of hanging out with a rock star who had attained cult status. This abuse of trust resulted in Cave's withdrawing from their company. Some of them therefore saw the album as the perfect opportunity to get even with him, not just as a public figure and performing artist, but also as a private individual. Falling victim to media plots is anything but rare in the superficial and fickle world the hacks inhabit and Nick Cave is by no means the only artist who has been done a disservice, but he was taken completely unawares. Only too well could he remember their deafening faultfinding, the ignorant way the entire music press had treated The Birthday Party, only to praise them to the skies once they had split up. Not all the critics were bastards, though. Indeed, some saw in 'The First Born is Dead' an ambitious project, but felt it was too wrapped up in itself and therefore too eccentric, an oddity, indeed. Cave, however, was legitimate in his assumption that the harmony of his music and lyrics on his second album was a huge leap forward and, to him, the bad press it received sounded hypocritical and two-faced.

The eight new songs on 'The First Born is Dead', resplendent in their blues and country arrangements, were a final departure from the wild days of The Birthday Party. It was slicker than its predecessor, and its self-restraint gives the album that special touch. Each track is a separate element within a cycle, the inter-dependence of each and every song bestowing on 'The First Born is Dead' the feel of a concept album, although that term had been contaminated by the art rock groups of the seventies that had used it ad nauseam. The opening track 'Tupelo' is set in the 'Swampland' landscape Cave had previously depicted on 'From Her to Eternity'. Tupelo, the birthplace of Elvis in the real world, here lies in an isolated valley. But doom and destruction are on their way. *'A big black cloud come! O comes to Tupelo.'* Thunder roars in the distance, the portent of a violent storm of biblical proportions. When it hits the town, the streets turn into torrential streams, the sun vanishes: *'Water water everywhere / Where no bird can fly no fish can swim / No fish can swim / Until the King is born / In Tupelo.'* A woman gives birth to two sons in a dingy shack, bails of straw its only comfort. Tragedy strikes when the first born dies: *'Well Saturday gives what Sunday steals / And a child is born on his brother's heels / Come Sunday morning the first-born's dead.'* Cave ingeniously juxtaposes the birth of Jacob and his younger brother Esau with that of Elvis Presley, who was born the second of twin brothers, his older sibling, Jesse Garon, dying shortly after birth. Taking up the narrative rhythm of Presley's 'In the Ghetto' where the legendary singer intones *'The snow flies / On a cold and grey Chicago morn / Another little baby child is born / In the ghetto'* Cave draws comparisons to the birth of Jacob, Father of the twelve Jewish tribes, and the tragic figure of the King of Rock. In Cave's 1984 draft for his novel which was nowhere near completion, the main character Euchrid Eucrow also survives his twin brother. The valley scenario he describes there, home to Eucrow, mute, of all things, is beleaguered by years of incessant rain. Euchrid, unloved and alone, is cast out by the townsfolk, the stage set for his murderous destiny. Just like the character in Presley's song who, also, never felt a mother's love, Eucrow grows up to be a delinquent with no chance of a normal life. It is an interesting by-line that Mac Davis, the composer of 'In the Ghetto', had originally entitled the song 'The Vicious Circle'. In August 1984, Cave had been giving public readings from his manuscript in LA and illustrated his reverence of the King metaphor to an even greater degree; for a short time he intended to entitle his novel-to-be 'King Euchrid'. Whereas 'Tupelo' eliminates the boundaries between fiction, intuition, and reality in a complex literary style, the music, composed by Adamson and Harvey, is influenced by a progressive traditional awareness. The bass, the melody to 'Saint Huck' played backwards, dominates the piece, while Bargeld's one-chord guitar shrieks in direct harmony. Yet it is the bleak male chorus of The Bad Seeds intoning 'Tupelo-o-o' that contributes most to the unique structure of the track, heralding the radical events that have yet to transpire.

Like 'Tupelo', the melancholic ballad 'Black Crow King' is also taken from Cave's manuscript. Here, Euchrid Eucrow, King of the Crows, is alone on a hill outside town, turning his humble abode into a fortress. *'All the hammers are a-talking / All the nails are a-singing.'* The incessant rain is

drenching the crows and their self-anointed sovereign has taken it upon himself to tend to the waterlogged harvest, full of hatred for the people who live down in the valley: *'You can hear it in the valley / Where live the lame and the blind / They climb the hill out of its belly / They leave with mean black shoes.'* Here, Nick Cave is speaking to those fans who took the religious imagery in his texts at face value, the 'crows' who would turn up at Birthday Party concerts armed with crucifixes, pointed black shoes and dark eyeliner. Is Cave, King of the Crows, also King of his Goth fans? The song, a slow blues ballad that almost stops in its tracks at times, is stripped to the bare essentials, held together by the backing vocals of the Bad Seeds and Bargeld's distorted guitar. Echoed by the band, Cave sings *'I am the King! The King of nuthin at all!'*

The track 'Blind Lemon Jefferson' again sees Cave in the familiar terrain of contrived biographies, events and locations. He sings the tale of a blind man who senses his time is just about up. Blind Lemon Jefferson makes his way up the street, the *'Tap-Tap-Tippin'* of his stick announcing his arrival, the crows impatient in the sycamore trees, *'they hop n bop n hop n bop.'* An outlaw, a loner, he's a man who never got to enjoy the finer things in life: *'O his road is dark and lonely / He don't drive no Cadillac.'* He remains a mystery, and the listener never discovers the reason for his gentle serenity. Blind Lemon Jefferson is one of Cave's most enthralling characters, the personification of the unknown, a mythical figure, more enigmatic than Saint Huck, Euchrid, and the legion of murderers the poet had so far breathed life into. Cave had written a 13-part short story in LA around about the same time as 'Swampland' and had condensed the intricate tale into the few bars of the song. He took as its inspiration the life of the American blues singer Blind Lemon Jefferson who was the most popular recording artists in the 1920s about whom little is known. Born in 1897 in Couchman in Freestone County, Texas, Jefferson died in Chicago at the end of December 1929 under strange circumstances. During his short life, he recorded forty-three 78's for Paramount which tell the story, in a vivid and colourful idiom, tongue planted firmly in cheek, of the incidents that befell him during his jaunts through the Deep South. Not quite what one would have expected from a black blind man at all. His life has never been fully documented, there being a distinct lack of reliable sources, so Cave makes up much of the detail, engrossed as he was by the mythical atmosphere of the 1920's and the mystery surrounding Jefferson's death.

Cave's short story is only remotely related to the real Blind Lemon Jefferson, but his character animated the author to new poetic heights. Meditating on Jefferson's blindness, he writes: *'Fear not, for he will not return your stare. See! They have put nickels in his eyes!'* Cave's Bline Lemon Jefferson is a drifter who earns his way as a reaper in the fields. One day, he receives the tragic news that his mother has died: *'Say, hey boss, mah poor mama's dead / Boss says he says Hey nigger if you don't get to work pronto, you'll soon be dead too!'* Bline Lemon Jefferson fells his boss with his scythe, steals his Smith+Wesson and flees over the border to neighbouring Arkansas, making sure to take his old guitar with him. Standing in the middle of a field, he starts to tell his sorry tale: *'Hay-rake hangin inna Boss-man's back / O Lawd have mercy on mah poor stinkin soul.'* Here, Cave is at his best. The band, too, excels – Bargeld's slide guitar and Adamson's bass complement each other, uniting with Harvey's percussion and Cave's mouth harmonica to give the song a modern feel, while never leaving any doubt that it is firmly rooted in the sounds and memories of the past. The remaining tracks on 'The First-Born is Dead', influenced by the fugue-like language of the old blues and the fiction of William Faulkner, are a fateful blend of Deep South myths, a parallel universe inhabited by honourable thieves, hillbillies, boilermen, slaves and preachers who innocently fall victim to the magnetic allure of murder, either out of love, desperation, or the fear of God. In this man's world, women are, at best, the source of inspiration, but more often than not, entice men to their doom with their beguiling ways, sealing their fates by simply coming into their lives. Or worse, women abandon them, crushing their spirits as they walk out the door, their broken hearts and sad laments their only solace. The tracks 'Say Goodbye To The Little Girl Tree', a bitter farewell, 'Knocking on Joe', the story of a man condemned to spent the rest of his life in a dungeon, fondly remembering his wife in her prime as he awaits death, and the elegy 'The Six Strings of Blood', the tale of a troubadour making a big mistake by playing a song for a girl, Rose, on his guitar as the mob comes to lynch him, all reflect the microcosm Cave creates with an insistence that borders on the obsessive.

The album also contains a second cover version, Bob Dylan's 'Wanted Man'. The original is a long euphonic list of all the places the outlaw of the title, a bounty on his head, can no longer dare show his face. Cave added a few extra lines and reworked the melody together with Harvey, thus turning the song into a tragicomedy with biographical undertones. Cave retains the basic scenario of the song, the Wanted Man having nowhere safe to go, but plays on his own celebrity status: *'If you love a wanted man, you'd best hold him while you can / Because you're gonna wake up one day and find the man you wanted he is gone,'* Cave suddenly intones, bemoaning the clichés of his life as a rock star who cannot afford to fall in love, no matter where his music takes him. Any artist who tampers with the intellectual property of another is legally obliged to inform that party of his intentions and must be granted authorisation before the work can be published. It is to Nick Cave's great credit that Bob Dylan, one of the world's most shy and retiring artists, personally okayed the Australian's reworking of his song. Even so, it took six months, during which time Cave and the Bad Seeds had to patiently wait for Dylan's legal representation to give the project the final go-ahead. 'The First-Born is Dead' was therefore released six months later than planned, but it was well worth the wait. The Dylan song didn't just fit in perfectly with the rest of the album, Cave had also received a rare accolade in being authorised to make changes to a composition penned by one of the greatest artists alive.

The six-month hold-up meant that Nick Cave and The Bad Seeds were forced to tour England in April 1985 without the material from the album the tour had been designed to promote. Even worse, Bargeld and Adamson had dropped out at short notice. Adamson didn't feel up to the heavy demands placed on him by his involvement with the band, and Bargeld was busy in the studio with Die Einstürzenden Neubauten. Harvey and Cave again faced the onerous task of finding replacements and thought it might be a fine idea to invite Thomas Wydler and Christoph Dreher of Die Haut to give it a go. And as fate would have it, Rowland S. Howard was invited to join them the night before. The band's performances were chaotic, and as one could have expected, Howard and Dreher for that matter, didn't really fit in. The tour was a mess and Cave's critics could hardly contain their glee. They still saw him as an unpredictable, journalist-baiting egoist who had dared to wander into the sacred grounds of the great country and blues singers. Just as Nick Cave had begun to show his artistic ambition to the world through his album and making himself vulnerable in the process, his critics were starting to label him as an arrogant, woman-hating, junkie bastard.

Many sometimes fail to see just how funny Nick can be.... I think he no longer has to hide behind his fantastically grotesque characters. They have courageously become himself.

John Hillcoat *(1999)*

LLULL, 145 - ☎ 309 18 89
08005 - BARCELONA

Vie es

23 Noviembre, 11 Noche

800 Anticipada
1000 Concierto

Incluída Consumición mínima

METRO: Llacuna - BUS: BSTP, 141, 71, 36, 40, 42

AND

Ghosts

How well I have learned that there is no fence to sit on between heaven and hell. There is a deep, wide gulf, a chasm, and in that chasm is no place for any man.

Johnny Cash

In 1985 Nick Cave sought refuge in West Berlin for the second time and remained in the city until shortly before the fall of the Wall in 1989. West Berlin was a long way away from the influence of the English press, and he was no longer being hounded by The NME or Melody Maker, magazines that were forever singing musicians' praises only to drag them through the mud when the mood struck them. Although he was still reeling from the attacks of the English media, the atmosphere in West Berlin couldn't have been more different. Nick and the Bad Seeds were well-known faces around town and their presence added a touch of cosmopolitan flair to the local underground scene. In Nick Cave's eyes, West Berlin was a city of opportunity. He now belonged to the in-crowd in the city's more notorious bars and was starting to feel quite at home. For years now he had been used to a life on the road, and material possessions hadn't held much interest for him. When, in the summer of '85, Cave was offered the chance of renting a small room in the flat Thomas Wydler shared with a few friends in Kreuzberg's Yorckstraße, he decided that having his own safe haven away from the hustle and bustle might do him some good. And at last, he would find some peace and quiet to get on with his novel. After the band's tour had ended the previous April – the one the English press had ripped to shreds – Cave invited Thomas Wydler to join the Bad Seeds as their full-time drummer. Wydler, whose talent had fitted in perfectly well with the band's general concept jumped at the chance, and he and Bargeld now formed a two-man German-speaking contingent in the Bad Seeds line-up. Mick had picked up German very quickly and was able to converse freely with his new colleague, but Nick Cave's knowledge of the language was still rudimentary. Enough to let him order vodka and beer at the bar in Risiko, but more importantly, it allowed him to avoid conversations he wasn't interested in.

In the mid 80s, the independent music magazine Spex was the top address for discerning fans in Germany. Spex recognised in Nick Cave the prototype of an ingenious class of musician who had crossed conventional borders. Readers voted in droves for Nick in the magazine's annual polls, invariably choosing him as 'Best Artist of the Year' who had played 'The Best Concert of the Year', had released 'The Best Album of the Year' featuring 'The Best Cover of the Year'. He couldn't help but be stirred by the loyalty Spex and its readers showed him. Greatly encouraged and with a new sense of purpose, the exiled Australian found the energy to dedicate a lot more of himself into his work during this welcome period of respite from the negative media coverage he had been getting outside Germany. As much as Nick Cave appreciated the recognition bestowed on him and his records by the West Berlin scene that had effectively turned him into a local hero, the simple fact was: Cave had just fallen in love.

Nick had encountered Elisabeth Recker the previous year on 21st May 1984 at a concert he played at West Berlin's Loft Club. Anita Lane thought Elisabeth's 'large nostrils' were an unmistakable sign of good character, and it didn't take Nick long to introduce her to the infinite joys of amphetamines. Gradually his feelings had grown stronger and he arrived on her doorstep shortly before he was due to record 'The First-Born is Dead' at the beginning of October '85. Recker was a well-known figure in the microcosm of the stranded Australians. She ran the Monogam record label that had released Die Einstürzenden Neubauten's first single, 'Für den Untergang / Stahlversion' a few years previously, the same label for which The Birthday Party had also recorded two songs in collaboration with Anita Lane. Elisabeth Recker was dedicated to her job and was utterly determined to earn enough to finance the periodic activities of her label. Although she was at the cutting edge of the business, she actually lived a rather ordered life, and unlike the vast majority of Nick's friends, Elisabeth had to get up early in the morning to go to work. The couple's dissimilar routines put a strain on their relationship to some extent and, of course, Nick's celebrity status certainly didn't make things any easier for them. His heroin addiction and the stress it involved made being the woman at his side difficult to say the least. Nonetheless, Nick and Elisabeth stayed together for nearly two and a half years and she proved to be the calming influence that had been missing from his life for so long. Elisabeth acquired an easy-going attitude to being a rock star's girlfriend, although she had to live with the macho sideswipes of those who believed that a more glamorous and less independent woman would have suited Nick better. In fact, never a day went

by without his putting pencil to paper and sketching some kind of smile-raising picture for her as proof of his affection. The pair became inseparable, only apart whenever Nick had to leave the city to go on tour with the band.

The autumn of 1985 was marked by several one-off performances and short tours of the United States, Australia, and Japan. The band played in Kyoto, Tokyo and Sapporo in front of audiences who saw the Bad Seeds, in their Bargeld-Harvey-Adamson-Wydler line-up, not as a loud excessive punk or rock band, but as a thrilling pop event not to be missed. The musicians were taken aback when Japanese girls started giving them teddy bears and bouquets of flowers instead of the drugs they were usually tendered. In addition, there was no being jumped on by raging punks looking for a fight, as had often been the case in other countries. After the Japanese tour finished in November, the band headed off for Australia to start recording new material for their next album and to do a three-week tour. Unlike the two previous Bad Seeds releases, for which Nick had written the lyrics and composed the music, this one was to be a compilation of cover versions of other artists' songs. Nick and the band had a whole list of favourites and on occasion had already performed some of them at their concerts. During their tour of Europe, Nick Cave and the Bad Seeds had played Nick's adaptation of Leonard Cohen's 'Avalanche', Bob Dylan's 'Knocking on Heaven's Door', the Elvis classic 'In the Ghetto', and Cave's innovative arrangement of Dylan's 'Wanted Man'. Screamin' Jay Hawkins' 'I Put a Spell on You' had been one of The Boys Next Door's standards, but as Hawkins, usually in a bad mood, was on the same bill as Nick Cave and the Bad Seeds in Australia, the song was dropped in favour of a number of other cover versions they had been hoping to try out. Harry Belafonte's 'Did You Hear about Jerry?' was much-loved as were Leadbelly's 'Black Betty', John Lee Hooker's 'I'm Gonna Kill that Woman', Johnny Cash's 'Muddy Water', and 'All Tomorrow's Parties' by the Velvet Underground & Nico. Nick Cave and the Bad Seeds wanted to see how these rock classics as performed in their superlative style would sound in front of audiences. After the tour, the musicians locked themselves into Melbourne's AAV-Studio and together with their sound engineer from old Birthday Party days, Tony Cohen, recorded 23 tracks in a very short time. Too many for one album.

Nick Cave's decision to include only other artists' material on the album, rearrange it and interpret it his way, was based on his curiosity to see if he could turn it into something radically new. Above all, it meant that he wouldn't be disclosing his personal emotions. Taking on country giants like Johnny Cash was a departure from music market logic which demanded that fans' expectations would have to be taken into account. Having spent months working several hours a day on his novel, the album would be a great challenge and absorbing himself in other artists' music would give Cave a unique opportunity to turn his hand to the great pop ballads of the sixties. A new album of Cave's own compositions would certainly have resulted in his having to bow to market pressures, something the artist simply refused to accept. Of course, countless other singers had recorded albums of other artists' material, but how many of them had actually managed to come up with something truly original? The twelve tracks on 'Kicking Against the Pricks' were needle-sharp and took a jibe at the music critics. Massive sales figures reflected that this album was out of the ordinary, instilled with an outstanding self-confidence. The spectacular way the songs are arranged has little in common with the originals, although the album is an exemplary homage to the band's heroes, albeit a controversial one. Cave chose songs whose myths and roots had been the foundation of many of his own compositions: the man who takes the life of his wife ('Hey Joe'); the man who declares his intention to murder his wife (John Lee Hooker's 'I'm gonna kill that woman'); the man who left his native valley after a devastating flood (John Bundrick's 'Muddy Water'); the man consumed by the fear that his wife's one-time lover could suddenly turn up out of the blue (Roy Orbison's 'Running Scared'); the innocent man stoically facing execution to protect his mistress' honour ('Long Black Veil' by Johnny Cash). And finally, The Seekers' hit 'The Carnival is Over', composed by Frank Farian, the man behind Boney M, is the sentimental farewell song of a man who has come to realise that he will never see his love again.

Inspired by the unique sound of Die Einstürzenden Neubauten, Cave freely reworked the Lou Reed composition 'All Tomorrow's Parties', the original version of 1969 a profusely euphoric hymn to drugs, and catapulted it straight into the 80s. Bargeld and Harvey are on guitar, their music distorted into an ear-splitting din. The two musicians complement each other layer for layer, creating an enormously accentuated intensity as they proceed. The chorus of the band tells the tale of a girl who flits from party to party in her pursuit of pleasure and recognition but is so lonely that she falls to pieces whenever she thinks nobody is observing her. Jimi Hendrix's biggest hit, the William Roberts composition 'Hey Joe', mutates into an ominous, impetuous experience in the Bad Seeds' good hands. Nick Cave's rendering is mellower than the Hendrix original, the arrangement combining feedback loops with a recurring bass piano rhythm and dramatic strings that suddenly surge up in a barrage of droning sound. As it takes on apocalyptic undertones, the text becomes grim *'Hey Joe where are you going with that gun in your hand? I'm gonna shoot my baby. I caught her messin around with another man.'* The relentless, furious resonance of these two tracks is at the opposite extreme from the tender, eternal ballads the band also covered on the album. Gene Pitney's 'Something's Gotten Hold of My Heart', The Seeker's 'The Carnival is Over', and 'Running Scared' are exceptional. Strings, acoustic guitars, a grand piano, and jazz drums balance the meticulous

precision of these tracks; however, it is Cave's empathic, compassionate vocals that wholeheartedly defeat the frequently affirmed criticism that the album was too commercial. Just like the hits of Frank Sinatra and Tony Bennett, these three album tracks reflect the soapier sound of the older generation. However, the Bad Seeds felt that it would have been sacrilege to pretend that these songs were anything else than sweet-sounding authentic ballads and made the decision to honour them as such. Cave sings the lyrics with a perceptible longing for true love, the heartache only a man who has loved and lost can recognise, and bestows on the song a kind of exaggerated sense of realism. He sings innocent couplets such as *'Like a drum my heart was beating / And your kiss was sweet as wine / But the joys of love are fleeting / For Pierrot and Columbine'* from 'The Carnival is Over' without even the slightest trace of cynicism, thereby retaining their simplistic beauty. About the same time as Nick Cave released his album of cover versions, Marc Almond issued his own version of 'Something's Gotten Hold of My Heart', which became one of the big summer hits of 1986. Almond's flat interpretation of this great classic serves to illustrate how seriously Cave took the original versions of the material he covered. He demonstrated deference for each of the songs on 'Kicking Against The Pricks' and the tales they tell. And in doing so, he took great pains to avoid any allegations of resting on other people's laurels, a pitfall many artists before him had been unable to avoid.

Cave used the album to pay tribute to the legendary American country singer Johnny Cash, whose comeback was still a decade off. He had been vilified by the media as the most iniquitous drug fuck-up in Nashville. What his detractors tended to disregard was that Johnny Cash had been the driving force behind the liberating of the C&W-Mecca from its reactionary image. Cave's respect for the Man in Black is reflected in his choice of three great Cash classics for 'Kicking Against the Pricks': 'Muddy Water', 'Long Black Veil' and 'The Singer'. These three songs form a spiritual link that fuses the album into a single entity. The opening track, 'Muddy Water', featuring Nick's mother, Dawn, on violin, is distinctive and bears witness to the relaxed and tension-free atmosphere in the Melbourne studio in January of 1986. The lines *'The road is gone, there's just one way to leave here / Turn my back on what I've left below'* are a poetic depiction of Cave's itinerant way of life. His rendition of 'The Singer' is much, much more than the mere interpretation of an excellent song; the track is the embodiment of Cave's own personal experience as it recounts the story of a figure who suddenly comes to grasp that his public has turned its back on him. Cave approaches the song as if it were a traditional air and, the strings of the Bad Seeds his only accompaniment, he intones: *'As I walk these narrow streets / Where a million passin feet have trod before me / With my guitar in my hand suddenly I realise nobody knows me.'* The words shout out their tragic truth, Cave's keen grasp of irony turning it into an indictment of the fickle world

FEBRUARY

australia

MARCH

6TH MARCH

APRIL

WEEK 1 →→ LONDON (Rehearsal)
" " 2   ENGLAND (on Tour)
" " 3   ENGLAND (on Tour)   → 6-7 DATES
" " 4 →   (HOLIDAY)

MAY

1 →→ AMERICA (on Tour)
2 →→ AMERICA (on Tour)   → 6-7 DATES
3
4 X WRITE NOVEL   (america)

FINISH BAD SEEDS

NICK CAVE LOVES ELIZABETH

JUNE

1 X
2 X
3 X   WRITE BOOK (america)
4 X
JULY   B

          B

YEAR 2045

outside: *'All the truths I tried to tell you / Were as distant to you as the moon / Born two hundred years too late / And two hundred too soon.'* When the single was released the last line of the song fell victim to the censor's knife, but *'Did you forget this fuckin' singer so soon? / And did you forget my song?'* is an emphatically accurate expression of Cave's own anger. Thus, whereas other artists might have been fearful of being reproached for their self-absorbtion in publicly displaying their vulnerability, Cave was able to lay down the gauntlet at the feet of his critics. The album cover, shot by Peter Milne, shows him posing in front of a red theatre curtain in a dinner-suit and bow-tie. Originally intending to call it 'Head on a Platter', he decided upon 'Kicking Against the Pricks', hoping that this more explicit title would be clearly understood by those it was designed to target.

While the rest of the band returned to London and West Berlin during the course of February, Nick and Elisabeth stayed behind in Australia and set off on an expedition through the South-East of the country. Its beautiful Pacific beaches were the ideal location to take some time out and relax. Nick was content just hanging out in the company of friends, although he did want to spend some time on a new project he had come up with and, before he returned to Europe, arranged to meet up with his old friend John Hillcoat in Melbourne, whom he had last seen in LA. The script for the impracticable 'Swampland' feature film had been gathering dust in Hillcoat's safe, but the director sensed that Cave's literary talent could be put to better use in writing the script of a full-length movie that could be realised technically with less effort. Both men had enjoyed Henry Jack Abbott's biography 'In the Belly of the Beast – Letters from Prison', the moving, true story of a criminal who had spent much of his life behind bars. In his autobiography, Abbott depicts in painful detail the unwritten laws of prison life: reprisals, violence, drugs, systematic humiliation, prisoner revolts, and the horrors of solitary confinement that replace the rule of law. On publication of the book, Abbott's publisher managed to get him a special dispensation, and, released from prison, he was feted by the crème de la crème of New York society as an exotic pop star. The in-crowd thought it would be cool to have a real live murderer in their midst, but Abbott was unable to completely adjust to living in the so-called civilised world. As if driven by an invisible force, he couldn't help but cross the thin line between the boundaries of lawfulness and unlawfulness. Naturally, the rules had all changed during his decades in prison, and the situation got irrevocably out of control in 1981 when Abbot murdered a waiter at a New York restaurant for refusing to let him use the guest bathroom. The city's elite, horrified, abruptly turned their backs on their reckless pet villain. Abbott was rearrested almost immediately, and, just like he had described in his book, people started baying for stricter legislation, more draconian sentences, and the total abolition of liberal prison regimes. In their eyes, the experiment had failed.

Nick Cave added a whole series of psychological character studies of inmates to the script Hillcoat and his associates, Evan English and Paul Goldman, had written at the end of 1987, as well as contributing several graphically depicted scenes. The film the Australians were planning to produce was entitled 'Ghosts … of the Civil Dead', and they cast Nick Cave in one of the major supporting roles. Fascinated by society's pariahs and killers, lost souls forever unable to put the crimes they have committed behind them, Cave relished acting out the finer points of the obstacles prison inmates are faced with. He approached the script from a socio-psychological angle that focused on the soothing influence of narcotics and that highlighted the illogical philosophy behind incarceration. Once inside the imprisoned lose their grip on reality, mediocre television and porn films their only contact to the outside world. In the film, Hillcoat portrays how the authorities take advantage of prisoners and their wardens as increasingly severe crime-busting policies are implemented and more funding is diverted into police work. 'Ghosts …' argues whether imprisonment is really an ideal form of punishment at all and throws open the question, objectively and without emotion, whether incarceration actually has anything to do with rehabilitation. The inference is that society locks up prisoners not to rehabilitate them but to throw away the key and put them out of minds. In 'Ghosts … of the Civil Dead', the main protagonist, Wenzel, is turned into a killer by the anxieties and pressures of being locked away in the high security wing of a fictitious Australian prison, while Cave plays the role of a hate-fuelled psychopath who upsets the delicate balance within the closed society his fellow prisoners have established, robbing them of their last scrap of dignity through his racist and denunciatory ferociousness. The film contains graphic scenes which show the extent to which drugs and extreme violence have become a part of everyday prison life. David Field, the actor who played Wenzel, hit the nail on the head when he described the ominous mood of 'Ghosts … of the Civil Dead' as *'The beauty of Ghosts… is that you see that violence is a personal thing, not something that only has impersonal consequences'.*

In March 1986, Cave set off for West Berlin in the company of Tony Cohen to put the finishing touches to 'Kicking Against the Pricks' in the city's Hansa-Studio. No sooner had they started work, Nick Cave and The Bad Seeds immediately ran into a spot of legal trouble. Cave and Cohen had been busy working on their unfinished tapes in the Richmond Recorders Studios in Melbourne, but insisting there were problems concerning unpaid bills, the studios refused to hand the final cut over for a few weeks. Mick Harvey maintains to this day that this strategy was blackmail pure and simple, and it left the musicians no other choice than to use their studio time in West Berlin to record new material instead. This unfortunate situation meant that, in August 1986, Nick Cave and The Bad Seeds were already working on a new album months before their previous one would be released. To make matters worse, Barry Adamson took them by surprise by jumping ship after the second recording session, maintaining that he was unable to cope with the inherent tensions within the band and had had enough of the constant personality clashes of its members. He subsequently returned to London and, with his sensational instrumental album, 'Moss Side Story', soon embarked on a successful career as a highly acclaimed soundtrack composer. The three remaining Bad Seeds were none too happy at Adamson's deserting them. They had worked well together and their chemistry couldn't have been more perfect. Now, musical inconsistencies were beginning to appear as a result of Adamson's defection, proving just how much he had contributed to the harmony of the band's sound. Blixa, Mick and Thomas had to come up with a way of making the best of a bad situation as soon as possible.

Harvey's and Bargeld's profile within the band was raised by Adamson's departure and they attempted to repair the damage the loss of their fourth pillar had caused in a new form of musical experiment. The result, 'Your Funeral … My Trial', was released in November 1986, only two months after 'Kicking Against the Pricks' had hit the record stores. As far as sales figures and the reception of the music press were concerned, the new album went tragically unheeded. Against all Nick Cave's expectations, 'Kicking Against the Pricks' had given rise to a complete change of mind within the English media. Journalists had forgotten all about their reaction to an album they had dismissed as the explicitly unruffled product of an overtly introverted artist. Cave was now being celebrated as a true upholder of serious music, as a connoisseur of the old school with a licence to put a new sheen on old songs. The interviews Cave had given in July to promote 'Kicking Against the Pricks' appeared as multi-page features in magazines all over the world, while pictures of the Australian star adorned their front pages. A tour to support the more than satisfactory sales figures had been scheduled for October and November and saw the band play gigs in twelve major European cities before setting off for the United States to give nine further performances in that country. Nick talked pianist Roland Wolf from West Berlin and The Gun Club's guitarist, Kid Congo Powers, into coming along as replacements for Barry Adamson and, above all, to give the band's sound a keener live feel. Mick Harvey, whose musical talents were apparently boundless, took over on bass, and the tour was a great success. The musicians had opted not to play any of their own old material with the notable exception of three great tracks: 'From Her to Eternity', 'Knocking on Joe', and 'Wanted Man'. The material from 'Your Funeral … My Trial', due to be released a few weeks after the tour ended, was also included in the repertoire, bar the two tracks 'Hard On For Love' and 'The Carny'. The rest of the gig was given over to the cover versions the tour had initially been designed to promote. During the European leg of the tour, the only incident of note was the band's disastrous concert at the Elysée Montmartre in Paris which there-

fore had ended in a brawl. There were, of course, the usual risks related to Cave's scoring drugs, but that was something everybody was used to. It all turned nasty in New York where Nick was arrested for possession – and had to cancel a VIP concert at the Ritz.

The music business has a deeply ingrained habit of viewing records as mere products and tours as simple marketing tools. Artists are treated as trademarks whose success is measured purely by the number of albums they sell. It is sheer folly for a record company to release two albums by the same artist within a period of only two and a half months. The label ought to ensure that there is an actual demand for a new album, thus guaranteeing a basis for earning revenue. Studio time and pressing is becoming more expensive by the year, so the ideal period between album releases is considered to be 18 months, sufficient to give the artist a chance to come up with new material, make a record, and go on tour to promote it. If a musician is lucky enough to have made the grade and has a loyal fan base in addition to a professionally-minded record company that knows how to do its job well, chances are that a new album will sell more copies than the last. For a singer like Nick Cave whose tours had already taken him to locations throughout Europe, the US, Australia and Japan, releasing a new album meant acquiring licences for some countries and meeting demand in others through exports. Whether an artist is minded to be involved in the marketing side of the business or not, as being the sole owner of the copyrights to his material, he is forced to play along with the intricate wheeling and dealing of the music world. Artists and producers spend a great deal of their energy booking studios, hiring session musicians, and co-ordinating flights and hotel-rooms. They have to bend over backwards to get advances from their record companies, arrange to reimburse them from royalties, and generally keep a beady eye on what the label is up to. Obtaining licences is a difficult and weary task, and mind-numbing discussions on fractions of a percent may go on for weeks before agreement is finally reached. Impatience can result in artists losing out on large sums of money, as the small pittance they earn on each album sale does eventually mount up. If an album is due to be released, marketing strategies have to be established and approved, journeys undertaken to sort through miles of red tape, and countless TV, press and radio interviews take their toll. In the evenings, musicians are expected to go out for meals with the directors of their record companies and music publishers, tours have to be booked and promoted, record covers designed, videos shot, and photo sessions scheduled. Photos and video clips are especially important, as they define the public's perception of an artist until the follow-on album is released, and any mistakes made at that stage cannot be put right. Artists have to incessantly sign mountains of paperwork, and the bureaucrats don't care whether an artist is on tour or if he is sicking a muse to help him come up with the right words to a heart-breaking love song.

When 'Your Funeral … My Trial' was released in November 1986, the approbation of the media towards Nick Cave had again dried up. Only true and loyal Nick Cave fans would have known that the new album had been released at all, and the unusual step of releasing it as a double 12" single was seen as confusing – it came over as a hybrid. It comprised eight tracks that were destined to be the end of Cave's blues phase for now. The first half of the album contains bona fide ballads, whereas the second has more of a rock feel. For the first time since the Bad Seeds had joined forces, he had managed to find a unique style that made the whole album stand apart. Influenced by motifs from his novel, which was nearing completion by the time the album was recorded, Cave's compositions were full of surprising forthrightness, especially on the track 'Hard On For Love'. Here, Cave sings from the perspective of a man who, driven by sexual desire, lays in wait for a young girl. The lyrics weave his arousal and self-doubt, the product of his religious upbringing, into a scenario overshadowed by a red moon, the portent of doom. *'The Lord is my Shepherd I shall not want / But he leadeth me like a lamb to the lips / Of the mouth of the valley of the shadow of death'.* The crime itself, murder or rape, isn't directly alluded to, thus implying that the scene may be all a dream or the fancy of a mentally disturbed man, dangerously high on sexual excitement: *'Her breasts rise and fall / her breasts rise and fall / Just when I'm about to get my hands on her'.* He approached the song from a radical angle, making it appear in a new and different light, particularly when seen from the viewpoint of Cave's novel. Euchrid Eucrow's motivation for taking the life of Beth, the young girl the superstitious villagers revere as blessed, is portrayed in a highly complex narrative. So, in 'Hard On For Love' Cave had condensed some of the elements from his novel into one single song. 'The Carny', the story of a circus troupe that loses one of its members during a stop-over in a remote mountain village, is supposedly taken from one of the original ideas Cave had for his book but didn't pursue. The atypical underlying glockenspiel, xylophone, organ and piano that characterise the song resonate in unison as the troupe buries the horse of their companion who has gone missing without a trace. On their departure, a cloudburst transforms the streets of the village into a raging torrent, a familiar metaphor in Cave's works, and as the circus performer's abandoned caravan sinks into the mud, the dead horse's resting place is desecrated and laid bare by the forces of nature, the crows swooping down on its carcass. The music on 'The Carny' may come across as slightly stilted, but its lyrics form a vivacious, intense representation of a mysterious episode, narrated in an idiom heavily influenced by the language of the Bible. Nick Cave unites in the song a whole series of elements that often crop up in many of his other compositions.

Tim Rose's 'Long Time Man' is the only cover version on 'Your Funeral … My Trial', and Nick Cave turned this popular '60s hit into an exemplary magical experience. He had not long finished reading Henry Jack Abbott's literary work and had spent much of his time working on the script for 'Ghosts … of the Civil Dead'. Hence, the choice of this song is all the more pertinent, as it tells the story of a man who shoots his wife dead in a town called Jacksonville and is sentenced to life imprisonment as chastisement. The song opens with the lines: *'Yeah, they came to take me away / said I'd be sitting here for the rest of my life',* fully mirroring Cave's recent prison study material. Embedded in a passion-driven rock arrangement, the prisoner sings of how the tragedy came to pass, why the quarrelling started, and how he finally reaches for his pistol, *'I can't even remember why',* putting an end to the argument there and then. The song was recorded with a truncated line-up, Thomas Wydler having injured his right wrist during previous recording sessions. Wydler could only look on as Mick Harvey took his place on drums. Cave's voice harrowingly describes the moment directly after the shot was fired, the protagonist's wife dying in a pool of blood on the kitchen floor: *'She looked up at me and began to smile / Her gasping words / Oh baby, I love you / Then she closed those baby blue eyes.'* As if music played loud can wipe away the memories, the Bad Seeds intone a seemingly relentless chorus that serves to accentuate the sheer tragedy of the song. 'Jack's Shadow' takes up the theme of Henry Jack Abbott's fate. Cave portrays Jack and his shadow as if they were a couple that has no stronger desire than to see the back of each other. In the associative language of his lyrics, the singer never reveals whether Jack sees his shadow as a stigma to be gotten rid of, or if it is more the malicious and constant reminder of being locked in a cell where the lights have never been turned off. Cave sings of how Jack is set free into the sunlight, but, still obsessed by outrunning his shadow, the first thing he does is get his hands on a sharp and dangerous knife: *'Said the shadow to Jack Henry / What's wrong / Jack said home is not a hole / And shadow you're just a gallows that I hang my body from / O shadow you're a shackle from which my time is never done.'* The sun beats down brightly as the shadow Jack so despised at long last fades away.

In musical terms 'Your Funeral … My Trial' saw Nick Cave and the Bad Seeds embark on a new path. The wonderful 'Sad Waters' and the album's title track are melancholy ballads that use the Hammond organ or the piano to their very best advantage, thus allowing them to carry the songs. 'She Fell Away', 'Jack's Shadow', and Bargeld's 'Stranger Than Kindness' prove that the band was still capable of greatness despite the chasm left behind by their former bass player. This holds equally true of the album's two rock numbers and 'The Carny', itself vaguely reminiscent of Kurt Weill. In their three-man incarnation, the Bad Seeds were able to find sufficient inspiration to create a sound that was at once full-bodied and vigorous. Bargeld's extraordinary atmospheric mode of expression on 'Stranger than Kindness' is defined by the multiple layers of his guitar chords. He was so taken by the sound he had created that he was to use similar arrangements in compositions for his own band, notably the song 'Fiat Lux' on the 'Haus der Lüge'. On Die Einstürzenden Neubauten's 'Fünf auf der nach oben offenen Richterskala' album, Bargeld even redefines Tim Rose's classic 'Morning Dew' as a steel-country symphony, a cover version that broadened the spectrum of his group. However, this process was by no means a one-way street. Nick Cave and the Bad Seeds learned much from Bargeld's style of playing the guitar and injected into their stage performances the vivacity their German friend, now on the verge of a major career breakthrough, had already fostered in Die Einstürzenden Neubauten. Bargeld was the principal force behind the industrial, icy reverberations that criss-cross 'Jack's Shadow', and his magnificent guitar distortions communicate the fundamental frantic atmosphere of 'She Fell Away'.

Four days after 'Your Funeral … My Trial' was released, just as the Bad Seeds had completed their American tour, Nick Cave and Mick Harvey received the tragic news that their friend Tracy Pew had died after an epileptic fit that had developed serious complications. Tracy had suffered his first attack about the same time a year previously, and his condition had been deteriorating as time progressed. The seizure of 7 November had brought on a fatal heart attack, leaving Nick Cave and Mick Harvey utterly devastated at having lost their best friend. Tracy was only 28 when he passed away, and his doctors confirmed that it was his illness that had killed him and not the excessive lifestyle he had so eagerly lived during all those wild years. Not that this was any comfort, and the feeling of loss ran deep. Suddenly, the two young musicians were confronted with their own mortality. Mick and Nick took a flight back to Australia to pay their final respects to a dear friend and colleague whose expertise on bass had last been heard on two tracks on 'Kicking Against the Pricks', 'Running Scared' and 'Hey Joe'.

1986 came and went. In early 1987, Nick Cave was still working on his novel when Wim Wenders, the German filmmaker, phoned him. Wenders, like Cave a Berliner-by-choice, was a big fan of Nick Cave and had been considering inviting him and his friends to star in a key scene to his film 'Wings of Desire'. Cave readily agreed. Nick Cave and The Bad Seeds were engaged to perform two songs, and filming was to take place at the derelict Esplanade Hotel on Potsdamer Platz, which, at that time, was a barren stretch of no-man's land on the border between East and West. In the film, two angels eavesdrop on the thoughts of the mortals Berlin is home to and record the events they have witnessed in the course of the day in their little notepads. In the evenings, the two angels tenderly read aloud to one another the observations each of them has made. Against all the warnings of his companion, one of the angels falls in love with a trapeze girl and makes up his mind to become human, willing to exchange his immortality for the imperfection of being a mere man. The Bad Seeds perform full-length versions of 'The

Carny' and 'Tupelo' as the trapeze girl then falls in love with the angel. The movie may come across as rather sentimental and perhaps pretentious, but the critics showed mercy and classed it as a fairytale-like epic. Its triumph at numerous film festivals was not only down to the tender love story it recounts, but also to the impressive backdrop created by Berlin as a divided city. 'Wings of Desire' was a big box-office hit, and Nick Cave's profile was enhanced considerably by his involvement. From then on, millions of cinema-goers began to link Cave's name to a film that had received the highest of accolades and was a highly ambitious manifest of the imagination of Wim Wenders.

Although 1987 had started off well, it was not to be a good year for Nick Cave. His heroin addiction began to dominate his thoughts to an increasing degree and for quite some time to come, he would not be in the right frame of mind to finish any of the projects he had started. The novel still wasn't ready for publishing, the jail movie had been bogged down in the initial phase, there was no question as yet of the Bad Seeds doing another album, and Cave's time-consuming literary obligations put paid to any ideas of them going on tour. Nick's private life was also a mess. He and Elisabeth Recker had split up in the meantime, and his new but rather obsessive manager, Jeanette Bleeker, had been making advances. But the fact was, Nick still missed Anita, although he had fallen in love with one of the girls he had met in Berlin. He simply didn't know where or who to turn to. However, Nick soon proved that he was made of sterner stuff, stoically managed to pull himself together, and threw himself back into his work. In June, he set off for London in the company of Mick and Anita and they recorded her first EP in the English capital, 'Dirty Sings' subsequently released twelve months later on Mute. Cave and Harvey recorded 'I'm a Believer', 'If I Should Die' and 'Sugar in a Hurricane' with Anita and Barry Adamson, and covered the Chic disco classic, 'Lost in Music'. The latter is remarkable in that it was the first time ever that the Australians had delved into the repertoire of the disco era, but Anita Lane's rendition, scaling the vastness between dignity and vulnerability, was eerily moving in its verve. Purely by a slight shift in the emphasis of the lyrics, Lane turned the song into a furious lament, removing any trace of the hymn to hedonism Nile Rodgers' original had been. In her version, the souls who are lost in music are also lost in life, her interpretation mirroring statements in interviews that she saw the songs on 'Dirty Sings' as a tangible manifestation of susceptibility, and not a quintessence of vigour and strength, as Cave's compositions usually are. Anita Lane's belated decision to use her own name for her debut release was only partly based on the fact that it is difficult for a woman to find acceptance in the chauvinist cliché-ridden rock scene. But in Lane's case she had been positively encouraged by Cave and Harvey to find a niche she could feel comfortable in. 'Dirty Sings' turned out to be a classic debut for Anita.

Back in Germany, Nick Cave spent the summer of 1987 in the city port of Hamburg where, after countless editing sessions with his friend Bronwyn Adams from Crime And The City Solution, he started to type his manuscript into a computer. He then embarked on the arduous task of revising it, only to ascertain that more work was required. The novel had become the main focus of Cave's life, and he had regarded his first public reading of passages from 'And the Ass Saw the Angel' five months previously, on 19th February, in the Deutsches Schauspielhaus in Hamburg as an important first hurdle. Though many of the Germans in the gallery hardly understood a word of his eloquent recital, the author was relieved that the rhythm of his prose seemed to sustain its flow before an audience. Above all, he had lifted the veil off his secret and to reveal that his ambitious project comprised a prologue, three separate sections, and an epilogue. The novel is set in the 1940s in a remote mountain-valley town and narrates the story of Euchrid Eucrow, a mute boy who lives with his alcoholic parents in a run-down shack outside town. Eucrow has been neglected by his unloving parents and is no stranger to serious beatings. His neighbours are no better and treat him like a worthless village idiot. Devoid of affection of any kind as he grows up, Euchrid seeks refuge in a vast swampland that soon becomes the main setting for his sorry tale. As a young man, he projects his dreams and fantasies on to Cosey Mo, a whore who lives in a trailer on a hillside at the edge of town. Mo is the only person far and wide who is not driven by the double standards and religious fundamentalism that otherwise mark the village. The valley's only source of wealth is the sugar cane that grows there, and when the area is beset by incessant rain for years on end, its citizens, deeply mistrustful members of the Ukelite sect, start to believe that God is punishing them for their sins. The charlatan Abie Poe gleefully convinces the cruel-natured villagers that the only way to stop the rain is to drive out the town's biggest disgrace: Cosey Mo. But even after she has been hounded out, the rain continues to fall, and the villagers vent their anger at Abie Poe. Nine months later, Cosey Mo dies, leaving the child she has just borne to a life as an orphan. Euchrid and his father are the only persons to witness Mo's lonely death while the Ukelites remain ignorant of the fate that has befallen her. The believers in the village are convinced that the infant is a divine messenger, as, when she is born, the rain suddenly stops. Gradually, Eucrow loses all grip on reality, steadfastly believing that the valley is cursed. Voices in his head lead him to become an angel of vengeance. After a grisly family drama and the resulting death of his parents, Euchrid's swampland retreat is accidentally discovered and destroyed by the villagers. This drives him to turn his parental shack into a makeshift fortress. He crowns himself King of his little empire and painstakingly prepares himself for his mission – to kill Beth, the now grown daughter of Cosey Mo. The narrative is fluid, deeply steeped in the imagery of Christianity and the sin of man. Cave's Eucrow firmly judges life on earth to be a purgatory.

Neither the misconstrued and murderous naivete of the protagonist's childlike character, the inability of any of the villagers to show pity or compassion for their barbaric acts, nor the ignorant visions of absolution that feature in the novel, are entirely convincing. A lack of authentic figures the reader can identify with defines Cave's fictitious world as a living hell where monstrous brutality, bloodletting and hypocrisy reign supreme. His literary debut is sombre with its explicit portrayal of festering wounds, the sadistic torturing of animals, and instances of dreadful psychological pressure, religious fundamentalism, not to mention the villagers' ritualised adoration of the Virgin, and thus far removed from any positive form of expression. Unless, of course, the novel's all-encompassing evil automatically arouses righteousness in the readers it tries so hard to repel. Nevertheless, Cave's novel is often brazen and can be read with ease for the most part, his choice of idiom making 'And the Ass Saw the Angel' more than vaguely reminiscent of the bible's most violent passages. Cave's imaginary dialect heightens the effect, but still, it appears that he may have been trying too hard in places. The novel suffers from the same factors that make it good: It was originally intended to be a movie script, and therefore Cave felt encouraged to change perspectives by introducing flashbacks, inner monologues, and parallel lines of events all too often. The anecdotes, legends and scenarios that Cave worked into his tragicomedy, however, are definitely enhanced by these cinematic heights that the author aspires to. Angles are too few but the novel is certainly tight and bursting with metaphor.

On 15 August, a month after he had started working on the final copy of his book, Nick and The Bad Seeds were scheduled to appear at the 'Kings of Independence' festival at Knopf's Music Hall in Hamburg, headlining a strong bill: Die Haut, The Swans, The Fall, Crime And The City Solution, and The Butthole Surfers. The organiser, Jeannette Bleeker, ecstatic about public response to the event, unforgivably sold more than double the permitted amount of tickets. When she announced that there wouldn't be enough room for several hundred ticket-holders, there was uproar and fans started rioting. The police cordoned the venue off, one group of fans trapped in the former cinema having to endure sauna-like temperatures for hours on end. Meanwhile, those who had not been granted entry were battling it out with the police on Hamburg's notorious Reeperbahn. The list of performers was long and it took ages to set up the stages, the festival obviously not having been too well-organised. The Bad Seeds were not due to play until five in the morning, and the unbearably high temperatures at the venue weren't exactly the best form of preparation for their set. An officially authorised live video of the festival featuring two of the band's tracks testifies to how excruciating being locked in the building for so long must have been. There is no footage whatsoever of the riots outside, as the cameramen were also locked into the building – it was certainly a night to remember.

In the course of 1987, the Bad Seeds only played twelve individual concerts, including shows in Ljubljana, Stockholm, Vienna, Turin, Athens and West Berlin. The Berlin performance was to be in celebration of the presentation to Wim Wenders of the Bundesfilmpreis and was the only known gig to have given illustrious high society guests the opportunity to hear the band's bonus track from the 'Your Funeral ... My Trial' CD, 'Scum' – Nick Cave and the Bad Seeds, of course, indubitably gave it their best. After this scandalous performance, Nick Cave then spent several months reworking his manuscript but still wasn't able to get it published. Eventually, on 7 September, the band got together to work on some recent material for another new album. Lacking concentration, without any direct recent experience of success, and constantly being forced to break off from recording due to Nick's drug problems, the band were having trouble making any headway. Work was held up for weeks in November 1987 as Cave headed off to Melbourne to film 'Ghosts ... of the Civil Dead'. Exhausted, plagued by bouts of paranoia, and aggressively high on opiates, Nick portrayed a constantly screaming psychopath, smearing his blood on to the walls of his cell.

Work on the album resumed in December and the musicians decided to later name it 'Tender Prey'. In the meantime, Mute had concluded that too much money had been wasted on too many takes that had been discarded, just like that, and were now expecting results. The entire situation was becoming a low-point in Nick Cave's increasingly worrying determination to self-destruct. This took on a completely new dimension when he was arrested in London for possession of 884 mg of heroin. He was freed on bail on the condition that he checked into a rehab clinic where he would be under constant medical supervision. This was an offer he certainly couldn't refuse.

I first met Nick Cave when I interviewed The Birthday Party for The Face magazine in the early Eighties. He had just been busted for drugs and was in a foul mood and was totally uncommunicative and horrible and quite funny: I was completely charmed by him. Tall, awkward and skinny, he was like a rude spider. We became friends when he moved to an unlikely house in Brixton (mock Tudor with a swimming pool) with his muse, Anita Lane. For the last 15 years he has been an unreliable but totally life-enhancing friend. His humour is more darkly sophisticated than anyone I know: he is one of the few people who can make me hysterical with laughter. He is a complete paradox: he is not at all influenced by other peoples opinions yet is deeply sensitive to criticism; he is acutely religious and entirely irreverent; he is simultaneously predictable yet one of the most original thinkers of his generation. His lyrics never cease to surprise me with their movement and beauty, and he is alone amongst his contemporaries in that his work has got better and better with age.

Jessamy Calkin *(1999)*

Gringo

When I was king / I made my rain / – but now my rain / Is made by those / Who carry keys / To walls and doors / Of brick and steel / – and memories.

Joseph Kallinger, 'Last Reign – Rain'

A typical characteristic of any crisis situation is that it can spread like a malignant growth and sap the strength of anybody who gets caught in its crossfire. By the spring of 1988, Nick Cave had still not been able to solve the difficulties he was facing in many areas of his life. However, despite the intense pressures he was under, Nick had managed to stick to the various projects he was working on, and after a one-week tour of Australia in February, the Bad Seeds were finally able to put the final touches to their new album in March. They had recorded the material in six studios in three different countries, and this patchwork method had left the band members drained and mentally exhausted. However, instead of taking things easy for a while, Mick Harvey, Blixa Bargeld, and Nick Cave started working on the soundtrack to 'Ghosts … of the Civil Dead' along with Anita Lane. After the bumpy ride they had had recording the ten new tracks for their next album, it was a great relief to be working on a well-organised project for a change, and there were a number of pre-set markers the musicians could follow, which made the procedure slightly easier. Much of the film was already finished, and the musicians found inspiration for their music in the heavy moods the completed scenes emanated. Thus, they were able to use to great advantage the film's superbly defined character motifs: the prison warden, the convict in solitary confine-ment, the transvestite, and the psychopath. Bargeld and Harvey had decided not to use any musical instrument typical of a rock band, and there are no Cave vocals on any of the tracks. Instead, the four friends created a composition totally devoid of feelings of hope, comfort and reconciliation, their sound insipid, and the moods

123

ominously underscored by strings and wind instruments. The wispy lenition of Anita Lane's voice is the only female element amid this claustrophobic prison environment – a raw and exclusively male world defined purely by mind-control and power games.

Although Nick Cave's detoxification at a facility in Weston-Super-Mare in the south of England was only a few weeks away, he gave into his cravings with relish. He was still preoccupied with the corrections to his novel, which saw him remove the many cumbersome terms and pretentious expressions from the manuscript he had painstakingly inserted over the last few months. Cave's deeper and deeper plunge into the world of his addiction was a last-ditch binge, before he was forced to turn his full attention to the course of therapy that awaited him. Many of the people who spent time with Nick Cave during those days later stated that he was a hair's breadth away from an overdose. In May, Nick was required to go over his book with his publisher, Simon Pettifar, a task that turned out to be a lot more time-consuming than expected. He turned his back on West Berlin, his home from home for very nearly six years, to return to London.

Cave stayed with friends who were sympathetic to the difficult situation he found himself in. While in London, a book of Cave's lyrics, entitled 'King Ink', was published. Much to his surprise, it received favourable reviews in the cultural sections of various English broadsheets. Nick Cave and the Bad Seeds subsequently played a one-off secret concert and were then scheduled to give four individual performances, one each in London, Utrecht, Amsterdam, and Hamburg in July. The band travelled in the same line-up as had recorded the songs for the new album 'Tender Prey', and was being feted by audiences and critics alike as the ultimate super group among the independent bands of 1988. In Mick Harvey (Ex-The Birthday Party), Thomas Wydler (Die Haut), Blixa Bargeld (Die Einstürzenden Neubauten), Kid Congo Powers (The Gun Club), and Roland Wolf, Cave had gathered around him an alliance of underground legends with years of experience and a hard-as-nails image. Their elegant black suits and shirts stood in crass contrast to their somewhat ashen faces. The NME journalist Jack Barron, who planned to write the cover story for the August edition of the publication in time for the release of 'Tender Prey', accompanied the band on their brief tour. Barron, constantly at close quarters to the musicians, soon located Nick's Cave's Achilles Heel, and, in an interview Cave gave him in Hamburg, kept pressing the Australian on his detox. Eventually, a massive argument broke out when Nick questioned what right Barron had to write about the impending treatment he was facing. The journalist had only discovered this information by accident and planned to publish it as a matter of his professional integrity, or so he maintained. When Barron then confronted the musician with the accusation that some of his friends had become addicted to heroin in imitation

of Cave's lifestyle, Nick finally lost his rag. Only two years previously, the Australian dailies had tried to lay the blame for a Melbourne teenager's suicide on Nick Cave because the poor soul had plastered the walls of his room with posters of his idol and had been listening to his records the night he killed himself. Like many celebrities before him, Nick reacted to the allegation of being responsible for the sudden and tragic death of a complete stranger with anger, furious at the hypocritical public procedures of the media machine. Barron's cover story appeared on 13 August with the sensational headline 'The Needle and the Damage done'. He describes Nick Cave as a monstrous junkie and even compares the venues the musician plays to the gas chambers of Auschwitz. Knowing that he had the upper hand and realising that it was his word against Nick's, Barron put his poison pen to paper and produced three obnoxious pages full of venom. He also denounced Roland Wolf as a heroin addict and wrote about him in a manner that was deliberately designed to portray his victim as an utterly ludicrous figure. The article was published while Nick was undergoing treatment and did nothing to improve the relationship between the artist and the press. Several years later, NME decided to republish the article in one of its anniversary issues, using it as an example of classic reporting – one of life's little ironies.

When 'Tender Prey' was finally released on 19 September, it was received favourably by most critics. The intensity of the songs, their musical directness, and Cave's clear-cut lyrics not only found acclaim in the music press, but were also being praised in celebrity lifestyle magazines such as 'Andy Warhol's Interview', 'Tempo' and 'The Face', publications that tended to make great use of colour spreads. However, the selection of songs on 'Tender Prey' which had received so much praise, is not unproblematic. Cave's previous albums had always been held together by a common thread, but 'Tender Prey', originally entitled 'The Ark', was a departure from this concept. If one considers artists' album releases as their published diaries or philosophical statements of stocktaking, everything Nick Cave had ever done can be taken as testimonies of confrontations he deemed inevitable. 'Tender Prey' is tinged by moments of distraction, is less focused than earlier albums, and the diary analogy is document to how much at a loss Cave felt at the time. This is not to say that the album was flawed, but Nick's sense of helplessness is distinctly conspicuous in the production. Cave and the band members had recorded nine good songs and one epic and forthwith declared this diversity to be the new way forward. The first single of the album, which was also its opening track, 'The Mercy Seat', is one of Cave's most intense pieces to date and falls in perfectly with the tours de force he had written in the past: 'Mutiny In Heaven', 'Sad Waters', 'Blind Lemon Jefferson' and 'From Her to Eternity'. Arranged as an incessant chorus, the song delves ever deeper into the question of guilt and innocence as it tells the tale of a convict on Death Row who, alone in his cell, is awaiting his imminent execution. Embedded within the Catholic idiom of sin and redemption and clearly inspired by his research into the lives of real-life delinquents, Cave describes the seat of mercy, the electric chair, as a shrine to absolution, the focus of the condemned man's thoughts: his one and only final certainty. The song comprises sixteen verses, the longest lyrics Cave had written so far, which describe the narrator's last thoughts, his quest for a formula to comprehend guilt as a philosophical entity and define his dignity as his sole remaining possession on earth. The song is a complex literary collage which again employs Bible imagery and motifs; after all, Jesus, too, was put to death. But in Heaven, Jesus took his place on His throne of gold, The Ark of the Covenant, the seat of His Will. In Cave's composition, the condemned man faces death on a less divine form of throne and, to muster courage in the face of death, he sings: *'And God is never far away'.* The Old Testament's concept of revenge which claimed 'an eye for an eye' and 'a tooth for a tooth' is compared to the age-old judicial equation that demanded a life for a life. From the eighth verse, deliberations are of no help, and the grisly sentence is finally carried out: *'Into the mercy seat I climb / My head is shaved, my head is wired / And just like a moth that tries to enter the bright eye / I go shuffling out of life / Just to hide in death for a while'.* Bound to the electric chair, the protagonist continues to sing from that point on from his new vantage position. Cave's literary technique has the first line of each individual verse subsequently depict the impending demise of his character. The agony of electrocution intensifies as the song progresses: *'The mercy seat is burning / And I think my head is melting'* – *'The mercy seat is glowing / And I think my blood is boiling'* – *'The mercy seat is melting / And I think my head is burning'.* But before the prisoner, fatigued by the trials and tribulations of his judges, declares, full of dignity and pride, that *'I'm not afraid to die',* he knowingly deplores his dead-end situation: *'And anyway I told the truth',* *'I've got nothing left to lose',* to conclude: *'And anyway there was no proof / Nor a motive why'.*

Four of the other songs on 'Tender Prey' are rock songs, two of which, the second single release, 'Deanna', and the up-tempo blues-rock number, 'City of Refuge', became a regular feature at Nick Cave and the Bad Seeds' concerts in the years that followed, as did 'The Mercy Seat'. 'City of Refuge' was briefly featured in the exclusively popular Peter Sempel music film, 'Dandy', which was premiered in 1988. The song is rather conventional and does not match up to the vigour and passion of 'Deanna'. Cave told various journalists, including Barron, that the latter was based on past events which had resulted in the break-up of his friendship with a girl called Diana. Any reporter who then asked about Diana was fed the same story: Cave and Diana, only eight years old, used to break into houses back in their native Wangaratta, stealing bits and pieces which they, as children, found interesting and discreetly trying out their victims' beds. On one occasion, Diana kept a loaded

gun she had found during a particular burglary. The Spex journalist Michael Ruff remembers Nick telling him: *'She's still on the Australian honours list of notorious juvenile delinquents for having shot two people dead. One day, she was caught in flagrante during a break-in and badly beaten up by the house owners: She returned later and shot them dead'.* For a short period, Cave even insisted that this was the reason why his parents had sent him off to Melbourne's Caulfield Grammar. However, realising that the four-year discrepancy between his version of events and actual facts would eventually come out, he sensibly consigned the story to the dustbin of history. 'Deanna' is still one of Cave's greats, even without any convoluted biographical investment, thanks to his stunningly pervading vocals and the murderous intensity of the music.

The mellower tracks, 'Slowly Goes the Night', 'Watching Alice', 'Mercy' and 'New Morning', benefit greatly from the sublime radiance that 'The Mercy Seat' and 'Deanna' emit. The three tracks were a continuation of the slower ballads of previous albums and Cave's preoccupation with covering the epic pop songs of the sixties. Consequently, they are firmly planted within the familiar structures the band had already tried and tested. The easy-listening arrangement on the captivating 'Slowly Goes the Night' harks back to the melodies of Burt Bacharach. Its perfectly timed rhymes reveal the generous gesture of a master who offers his audience some gentleness and tranquillity. In 'Watching Alice', Cave, accompanied by a gentle piano melody, narrates how, one June morning (like every morning, *'year after year'*), the singer secretly watches a woman getting dressed. But Alice is a dominatrix putting on her leather uniform, and, to the sound of a lamenting harmonica, the voyeur intones with ironic empathy: *'Watching Alice dressing in her room / It's so depressing it's true'.* This little excursion into the realm of sarcasm gets its point across before being followed up by 'Mercy', in itself a bow to God. As if driven by some unseen force to condense the most blatant religious clichés into one, Cave implores in language taken straight from John the Baptist: *'Thrown into a dungeon / Bread and water my portion / Faith my only weapon / To rest the Devil's legion'.* Only prayer can help as Cave dramatically intones: *'And I cried Mercy / Have Mercy upon me / And I get down on my knees'.* 'Mercy' is an excellent song and creating splendour through the beautifully tragic musical humility Roland Wolf contributed. The Bad Seeds and Nick Cave form a chorus begging for mercy with such ardour and force the musicians had never before had about them. Nick Cave's aspiration to try and broaden his horizons as an able singer of moving ballads is reflected in his successful rendition of the song. 'New Morning', the final track on the album, was intended to be performed as a gospel song, a prayer to God who has led the singer to enlightenment. One morning he wakes up and … *'A new sun was shining.'* Nick Cave and the Bad Seeds sing in praise to this new morn: *'There'll be no sadness / No sorrow / No road is too narrow / There'll be a*

new day / And it's today / For us'. Cave, one of the few brave great admirers of Bob Dylan's misconstrued religious albums, had done his homework well. In 1978 Dylan had converted from Judaism to Christianity and had published two albums of gospel songs, 'Slow Train Coming' and 'Saved'. Years later Cave was to admit in Mojo magazine that 'Slow Train Coming' was *my all-time favourite album (…), full of mean-spirited spirituality. It's a genuinely nasty record, certainly the nastiest Christian album I've ever come across.'* He knew that only the ignorant would jeer at songs that sang the praises of the Lord. He also recalled that, for many years, Bob Dylan had had a habit of radically changing styles on the last track of his albums, thereby hinting at what he might be coming up with next. Nick Cave would do the very same thing a year later, but in the meantime, 'New Day' was destined to become the final encore at many Bad Seeds concerts from then on.

Three days after the worldwide release of 'Tender Prey', Nick, now 31 years of age, was released from his incarceration, and the hell of his heroin detoxification programme had visibly taken its toll. He had added the sobering experience of unbearable physical and mental pain to his long list. Now, for the first time since his youth, Nick was clean. Having survived his only alternative to jail, he was now thrown into a brand new life. The Australian ignored the advice of his doctors and counsellors who strongly warned him against setting off on a three-week tour with the Bad Seeds only seven days after his discharge from the clinic. They had justified concerns that the tour and its hectic rock'n'roll environment would be too much of a temptation for their former patient who had just set out on a new path to abstinence. There would certainly be an abundance of drugs going around, so, of course, these doubts were well-founded. From a long list of concerts, fans usually only see one specific show and then return to the routine of their everyday lives. They are glad to have had the chance to see an inspired performance by their favourite artists and may feel let down if the long-awaited event turns out to be lacking. If a fan wants to see an idol close-up, he will head for the often dreary dressing rooms, if the bouncers don't stop him, he might get lucky, even helping to consume the stacks of alcohol that have been provided by the organisers for the band's whole entourage. Having given himself the honour of attending a party someone else has paid for, the fan will depart into the night, his personal notions of what touring with a band is like, safely confirmed. Special occasions are for fans what routine is to the band.

The artists may be on a long journey that started at some point in the past and it may have a long way to go yet. Musicians might have to set off in an overnight bus for their next destination as soon as the post-concert frolics have ended to arrive at some other club in yet another unfamiliar city to do it all again. If they don't have all that far to go, they may stay overnight in hotel-rooms that look frighteningly like the previous ones. This mind-numbing routine explains why longer tours quickly lose all of their glamour. Days and nights, whiled away in coaches, planes, and trains, are spent in wait and are at the opposite extreme to the thunderous noise and energy of their concerts, the baying fans, and the welcome release of pent-up emotions. The temptation to enhance the crescendo of a concert by taking drugs is overwhelming for somebody who knows exactly what the substances do for you. It was precisely this kind of excessive lifestyle that Nick Cave had pursued for many years regardless of his health.

Nick had resolved that not succumbing to temptation was a test he had to pass with flying colours if he wanted to continue his career as a musician. True to form, he managed to muster enough inner strength to resist the former object of his desire. The Bad Seeds' new tour manager, Rayner Jesson, had begun to exert a subtle kind of psychological influence on Cave and understood how the Australian must have been feeling. Much to everybody's surprise the former junkie's will was stronger than anyone had believed, in fact, it turned out to be as solid as rock. There were no negative incidents at all at any of the 17 concerts the band played in September and October in Finland, Denmark, Germany, Holland, Switzerland, Austria, France, and then back to England to perform at a sold-out Town and Country Club over two nights. Three months later, in February 1989, Nick Cave and the Bad Seeds were accompanied on their tour of the United States by the Berlin student of cinematography, Uli M. Schüppel, and his sound-assistant, Lucien Segura. Schüppel was an old friend of the band from their Berlin days and had devised an ambitious plan for his final exams at the film academy. He wanted to shoot a documentary about Nick Cave's American tour in the style of D. A. Pennebaker's revolutionary Bob Dylan films, 'Eat the Document', and 'Don't Look Back'. With the Bad Seeds' authorisation, the filmmaker intended to capture the everyday situations that accompany a tour rather than too many concert scenes, and hence managed to record for posterity a number of bizarre moments: fans who, finally face-to-face with their idols, are absolutely gobsmacked, or loud arguments with venue directors who had installed inferior-quality amplifiers to save money. In the opening scene, Nick is shown leaving the dressing room to go on stage and practising the lines: *'Three things: I'm Nick Cave. I Love you. And I wanna tell you about a girl'–* only to repeat them shortly afterwards to the audience. To lighten the mood during endless bus journeys through dried-up salt lakes, industrial zones, and sandy deserts, Cave and Harvey would sing melancholic country and western songs, including one called 'The Road to God Knows Where', the title Schüppel chose for his documentary. The film itself is full of associate narrative rhythms similar to those in 'Don't Look Back'. It successfully documents the humdrum of life on tour and has an intense sense of poignancy for absurd situations while preserving the intimacy and privacy that had rendered 'Eat the Document' so exceptional. Even if the black-and-white production is technically flawed in places, such as when the sound engineer, Segura, initiates conversations with those present in the scenes shot backstage, nonetheless, 'The Road to God Knows Where' is an atmospheric piece of work in a genre which has produced only few masterpieces over the last decades.

When the American tour had ended after the last gig in LA, Nick Cave returned to London to make the final set of corrections to his novel in collaboration with his publisher. A great weight was lifted off his shoulders of the recently sober star after seven long years of sporadic activity on his literary work. He had lost numerous hand-written hard copies of his book in the past and had unfortunately not bothered to make replacements. Many other literary novices, faced with such massive setbacks, may have simply capitulated. However, Cave tended to believe that, as a mere rock star, he was at the bottom of the artistic ladder, and was driven by the fear that his literary ambition would be ridiculed. Experiencing adversity, he had always managed to pull himself together and continue with his novel full steam ahead. Even his publisher, Simon Pettifar, couldn't really be angry at his protégé's submission of his finished manu-script a year later than expected, because 'Tender Prey' was a great commercial success. This helped the novel to sell surprisingly well when it was at last published at the end of the summer − bearing a dedication to Anita Lane. *'In 1998 we started earning real money, for the first time since we had left Australia',* Mick Harvey recalls, *'but it didn't spoil us, as we saw our financial success as a confirmation that the path we had chosen was the right one'.* No longer dependent on drugs and liberated from the burden of writing his novel, Nick's future as a musician was looking bright. He had fulfilled a dream he had long nurtured and, along with the Bad Seeds, jumped on a plane and headed off in the direction of a country he had always wanted to see but had never had the opportunity as yet to do so: Brazil.

Scheduled to play two gigs at the Projeto São Paolo venue on 14 and 15 April, the whole band was dumbfounded by the sheer geographical dimensions of the Brazilian metropolis where fate was about to throw Nick Cave together with his future love, artist and fashion designer Viviane Carneiro. Thomas Wydler remembers: *'We went to the Copacabana in Rio first of all and, two days later, arrived in this gargantuan city. It was a completely different world. Nick totally changed and started to absorb the sound of the lan-guage around him and sucked up the atmosphere of that amazing city. Then, suddenly, he fell head over heels with Viviane'.* Nick extended his sojourn in Brazil to spend two more weeks with Viviane and made his mind up during his extra fortnight in the country to move permanently to this city of 16 million whose sprawl crept out towards and over the horizon. However, there were a few obligations he had to see to first and, love-sick and with a heavy heart, Nick returned to his old world and to set off on a tour of Italy and Japan. As public readings of his novel and interviews to pro-mote the book would also keep him in Europe during July, August, and September, he made the hazardous decision to record the Bad Seeds' next album in a studio in São Paolo so that he could spend more time with Viviane. The five long months the couple had been compelled to spend apart due to Nick's tight and demanding work schedule now brought the lovebirds even closer together.

With his move to Brazil Nick Cave embarked on a new direction in his life and, for the first time ever, started to live a semblance of an ordered existence. Of course, the Brazilian media had taken note of the fact that an internationally renowned pop star had chosen to live in São Paolo, and it didn't take long before Nick Cave's face was splashed over the front pages of various dailies that also dished up the dirt on his career and his private life. But in the ano-nymity of this colossal city that spoke Portuguese and not English and where rock music hadn't become the kind of ersatz religion it had in England, Cave didn't feel at all impinged upon by the interest Brazil showed in him. Although he didn't have any reason to sub-scribe to the Brazilian way of life, the country was the perfect place to get away from it all, because it was principally an exaggerated melange of football, cocaine and carnival. The sun always shone, the Catholic attitude of the people cast a spell on Cave, and the architecture, ancient and new, was breathtakingly beautiful. And, of course, there was Viviane. Life was starting to look as if it might become much more pleasurable and satisfying than it had been for a long time. Nick was greatly relieved when he came to realise that having given up drugs for good didn't appear to be putting the dampers on his creativity. Moreover, the experience of writing his novel had successfully exorcised all of the demons that had taken precedence in his literary work and his songs for so long. The path ahead therefore was now clear for new forms of artistic expression. Back in Europe, the Bad Seeds had recorded nearly enough material for a whole new album, which, in itself, was a turn-up for the books. During his time with The Birthday Party and since the beginning of his solo career, Cave had usually passed vague ideas for songs on to the members of his band who then polished up the arrangements. Based on mere concepts of how the finished album should sound, the final versions of many of Nick's latest compositions comprised the sum of all of the musi-cians' enthusiastic ideas and suggestions. Suitably briefed, Kid, Blixa, Thomas, and Mick arrived in São Paolo in October to record the new album, 'The Good Son'. Roland Wolf didn't join them as artistic differences had led to his exclusion. Totally unlike the work the Bad Seeds had done on 'Tender Prey' a year previously, the band, this time, made good progress, as each of the musicians was perfectly familiar with the individual tracks they were to record. The only major hold-up was the inferior technical standard of the Cardan Studios that had been booked for them in São Paolo. The piano didn't sound like a piano on the tapes and had to be re-recorded in Berlin a few months later when the album was being mixed by Flood and Gareth Jones.

The band thoroughly enjoyed the time they spent living in Brazil. Their hotel was close by the studio – and Pedro's Bar, where they could buy delicious Caipirinhas and other scrumptious cocktails – an unending source of good cheer. Moreover, the musicians were absolutely astounded by São Paolo which was quite unlike anything they had ever witnessed in Europe, Australia or even California. The come-to-roost musicians were infected by the contagious impulsive mentality of the Brazilians and their intense warmth, but were able to cool down in the air-conditioned environment of the studio and did an excellent job on 'The Good Son'. The songs the musicians recorded in Brazil are marked by a relaxed mood of timelessness that was enhanced by their exotic surroundings. São Paolo is a vast city of modern office skyscrapers that have shot up among the centuries-old colonial architecture of the city centre, all of it bleached by the heat of the sun. Brazil's economy was rather shaky and the state itself corrupt, but Nick Cave and the Bad Seeds were very impressed by the way people took life there. 'The Good Son' is the second Nick Cave album after 'Kicking Against the Pricks' to achieve classic status, down to the exuberant charm radiated by each of the individual tracks. The delectable strings and the enticing sounds of a grand piano combine with stirring acoustic guitars, and the ballads and soundtrack-like compositions on the album are testament to an affability and reconciliation that had never before been so evident in Cave's previous compositions. Above all, he recorded these out-and-out pop songs with an unusually well-oiled voice, and the refrains are so memorable – in the way children's lullabies are – that, once heard, they are never forgotten.

The opening track 'Foi na cruz' sets the tone for the whole album. Cave worked the traditional Portuguese anthem of the same name into his song: *'Foi na cruz / Que um dia / Meus pecados castigos em Jesus'* *('He hung on the cross / One day / Jesus was punished for our sins')*. Cave had heard the air for the very first time in the 1981 award-winning film 'Pixote' by director Hector Babenco ('The Kiss of the Spider Woman'). The film recounts the sorry life of Pixote, a ten-year old street urchin, who breaks out of a young people's sanctuary ruled with prison-like discipline, to end up as a drug-dealer in the urban wasteland of the metropolis. Nick was enthralled by the sheer suffering of the film's main character, especially when he discovered that the child actor's fate had become a mirror image of the character he had played as a young boy. Ferdinand Ramos da Silva, the actor in question, never got the chance to grow to maturity as, two years previously, the São Paolo police had shot the now seventeen-year-old in a near execution, putting a tragic end to a short life.

Cave had already dedicated 'Tender Prey' to da Silva, who, in one scene of the film, sings 'Foi na cruz', accompanied by a street preacher and a small crowd of people. In Cave's adaptation of this traditional air, he adds the old Portuguese refrain to the verses he composed himself, where he sings the woeful tale of how two people missed a golden opportunity to fall in love *('Love comes a-knockin / Love comes a-knockin on our door / But you, you and me, love / We don't live here anymore')*, which may also have been meant as a gentle tribute to a highly gifted human being he was destined never to meet.

Until that time, Cave had often been wont to write complex, intricate stories with equally complex linguistic structures. Songs like 'Foi na cruz' are therefore all the more fascinating because of their simplicity, their loose associations, and the secrets they allude to but never wholly divulge. The songs on 'The Good Son' are steeped in a sense of pronounced melancholy and loss for which the Portuguese language has a fitting term: 'saudade'. This ethereal mood can be found at the very core of Brazil's popular music, from the bossa nova to the fado. For Cave, these musical styles had been a minor source of inspiration; he had dedicated himself more to the melancholy and mystery that singers from the northern hemisphere summoned, such as Van Morrison on his 'Astral Weeks' album and Bob Dylan on 'John Wesley Harding'. The album's title track, 'The Good Son', for example, describes the fate of the good son who hates his parents and his brother and subsequently does away with them. He works as a tiller, which has the ominous ring of the word 'killer'. The song couldn't be further removed from the abrasive blues references so frequently found in much of Cave's earlier work. Instead of inflating the story into a cathartic extreme embedded within a spartan but ear-splitting instrumental accompaniment, the melodramatic mood of 'The Good Son' and of the love song 'Lament', with its strings and theatrical chord changes, remind the listener more of compositions by Ennio Morricone. 'The Weeping Song' is Nick Cave's duet premiere, arranged as a dialogue between a father, sung by Blixa Bargeld, and his son, sung by Nick Cave. The son is driving his father to distraction by forever asking why men and women are always crying. The verses of the song are exemplified in the lines: *'Father, why are all the women weeping?' – 'They are weeping for their men' – 'Then why are the men there weeping?' – 'They are weeping back at them'.* The father himself starts to weep as his son refuses to grasp that it is life itself that offers humankind no other choice than to shed their tears in a constant flow. The humour that is inherent in Cave's compositions is also perceptible in 'The Weeping Song' but is expressed in a very subtle way behind a mask of fatalism. 'The Witness Song' is the only track on the album to deal with Nick's experiences during the time he spent in rehabilitation in England and is a rare auto-biographical revelation of sorts. The song, put across as a fairytale, tells the story of a couple. Without any trace of cynicism, the singer refers to the woman as his 'friend'. The couple emerge from a fog and walk into a spacious but overgrown garden with a sacred fountain at its centre. Both drink from the water, but the healing it brings forth marks the final step on their common journey. When the singer takes leave of his partner, an obvious reference to Anita Lane, she raises her hands to her face and turns away, her motion illustrating her hurt. Cave sings: *'That gesture, it will haunt me'.* Anita had returned to be at Nick's side during the difficult weeks after his enforced sojourn at the clinic and had been a great source of strength. However, Nick's decision to move to Brazil to be with Viviane thus also signified the finality of his break-up with his former lover.

In many respects 'The Good Son' was also the start of a journey into unfamiliar terrain. The songs on the album allowed Cave to adapt all the great gestures of the heartbreakers, troubadours, and crooners before him into a much more dramatic form of expression. In the video for 'The Ship Song', again, shot by John Hillcoat, and on the album cover, Cave can be seen posing in a white suit, surrounded by little girls in ballet costumes, his black grand piano shining like a new pin. The playful manner of his handling of the insignias of show business is recognisable in his ironic over-exaggerated style, and this theatrical gesture hit the mark. Music publications all over the world started wondering whether the one-time punk idol had sold out and had betrayed his fans. The only saving grace that Nick Cave could see was that his hero, Bob Dylan, had been accused of the same crime on numerous occasions but had always emerged for the better from such conflicts and, hence, learned how to defend his integrity from attack. Dylan had had to endure the scathing tongues of those who believed they had a God-given right to call the shots on his musical steps forward. Fans had drowned him out with loud whistling and heckling at his concerts when their hero had turned his back on folk to concentrate on rock music. The same thing happened when he abandoned rock to record a country album with Johnny Cash, not to mention when he had come up with the idea to approach his songs from a Sinatra-esque standpoint, accompanied by a female choir. Despite these venomous condemnations, Bob Dylan had always managed to regain his standing, his steadfastness and self-belief allowing him to achieve a heroic outlaw status. Nick Cave's career wasn't too unlike Dylan's in this respect. The Australian had also seen his fans react with disappointment to 'The First Born is Dead' when he had left the wild days of The Birthday Party behind him. He had delved into the depths of melancholy for 'Kicking Against the Pricks', and, now, 'The Good Son', with its mature simplicity, had represented the biggest style change Cave had ever dared to make. However, this time Nick was supported by the loving woman at his side, and his critics were thousands of miles away from the tension-free

atmosphere of Brazil. His audacity was more than rewarded: 'The Good Son' was released in April 1990 and the 250,000 copies that were sold soon turned it into the most commercially successful album Cave had ever recorded, even reaching the number one spot in the charts in Greece and Israel.

Nick Cave and the Bad Seeds were scheduled to play 49 concerts between May and October, taking in venues in Europe, Japan, Australia, and the States. The singer was therefore able to substantiate his newly established status as an underground superstar who had successfully managed to create something unique by utterly detaching himself from contemporary music trends. The concerts were given without the participation of Kid Congo Powers, as the tour had clashed with his busy schedule with The Gun Club. To replace him and to find someone to take Roland Wolf's place on the organ, Cave invited the Australians, Martyn P. Casey of the Triffids, and Conway Savage, to accompany the Bad Seeds on their journey around the globe. As Casey was proficient on bass, Mick Harvey was able to reassume his role on lead guitar, a charade that became more permanent. Bargeld, Harvey, Wydler, Casey, and Savage would from now on form the pillars that carried the band for years to come. Cave's profound interest in traditional musical structures, which had now been made public with the release of 'The Good Son', also transformed the way the band portrayed itself. Liberated from the self-destructive image of a performer whose concerts had been expected to end in excessive horror trips, Cave used his new-found freedom to try out a variety of interpretations of his songs, thus injecting a new sense of dynamism into his concerts. Nick Cave's life utterly changed with the birth of his first son, Luke, on 10 May 1991. Having to assume responsibility for a family, while being showered with the innocent purity of the love of his new-born child, compelled the Australian to redefine his priorities. Nick had lived the life of a rock musician for so long, and having advanced to the status of a star over the past few years had seen him direct most of his energies into his persona as a performer. Now as a father, Nick began to compose lullabies he could sing to Luke in the evenings. 'Papa Won't Leave You, Henry', one of the most touching, a version of which was released a year later on his seventh solo album, 'Henry's Dream'.

Along with his continued global success, Nick Cave's working routines took on new methodologies. He had usually released albums every twelve months or so, but now it was taking twice as long. The longer periods between releases were down to a number of factors, taking life easier only one of them. Nick was spending much of his time with Viviane and Luke in São Paolo, and the tours he was contractually obliged to do were more time-consuming than he was accustomed to. As a consequence, the Australian simply no longer had as much time to sit down and put his mind to writing songs. The individual members of the band were also busy working on their own projects and had been invited to contribute to the soundtracks of various films, including Wim Wender's 'Until the End of the World'. They were also commissioned to assist in compilations of other songs and recorded the Neil Young track, 'Helpless', for an album tribute to the American that was planned to be released, entitled 'The Bridge'. Nick contributed an extraordinary version of 'Tower of Song' to the album 'I'm Your Fan – The Songs of Leonard Cohen'. Its extroverted stylistic reverberation had method: the musicians recorded several takes during one long session without rehearsing the song beforehand. They then took various aspects from each of the takes and subsequently mixed them into the finished track. Cohen was impressed and, shortly afterwards, a thirty-minute version was incorporated on the illegally released bootleg, 'More Pricks Than Kicks'.

In 1991, Nick appeared in Tom DiCillo's Hollywood comedy, 'Johnny Suede', in a supporting role alongside Brad Pitt. The latter plays the title character, a young man sporting suede winkle-pickers and a gigantic quiff. In the film, Johnny Suede dreams of becoming a celebrity rock star, and his gauche endeavours to climb the ladder of stardom are superbly depicted, as is Johnny's affair with a paranoid girl and his subsequent falling in love with a kindergarten teacher. In this gentle satire on the James Dean films of the '50s, Cave is cast in the role of a sinister rockstar who goes by the name of Freak Storm, with a quiff and winkle-pickers even more impressive than Pitt's. In one of the film's grotesque key scenes, Freak Storm can be seen giving advice to his young admirer, singing several lines from a dizzying, fully over-the-top song, 'Freak's Mama Boy', before forcing Johnny to eat a piece of chicken that has outlived its sell-by date, a fact he neglects to tell Pitt's character. In interviews given after 'Johnny Suede' was released, Cave stated that he wasn't amused when the producers cut the Australian's favourite scene from the film. It had shown Cave licking the armpit of a beautiful woman, an improvised replacement for a lack of salt to accompany his tequila. The role could have been written for him, and his debut as a Hollywood actor was less of a feat than for many. Above all, Cave was now being recognised in New York and LA as a celebrity, because he had done a movie with the illustrious Brad Pitt. Nick, Viviane, and Luke had left Brazil for the US in October '91 as they didn't want to be apart during the shooting of 'Johnny Suede', and, as the band had decided to record their next album in that country, Cave took an apartment in Manhattan he and his family could feel at home in.

For the first time since the Boys Next Door fiasco, Cave decided to work together with a producer during his extended stay in the US. Unlike sound engineers whose main task is to ensure that the music played during a studio session is actually recorded on tape, the influence of a producer on the recording process is enormous. A producer will propose the choice of studio and will decide on who to hire as sound engineers and technicians. Famous producers assume responsibility for seeing that things go according to plan and find ways to keep a particular artist or band on the right track. In Nick Cave's case, Mute was hoping that the musician would be able to make a bigger name for himself in America with his imminent new album, as he hadn't quite made the grade there yet. Moving to New York was a first step, hiring David Briggs a more momentous second. Briggs had already worked on a whole series of Neil Young albums, including 'Zuma', 'Rust Never Sleeps', 'Re-Act-Or', and 'After The Goldrush', and had managed to find fame through their rough and ready sound. For Cave, the idea that an album of his might sound like one of Neil Young's classics was appealing and weakened his otherwise cautious stance towards being artistically manipulated. At the same time, Briggs's role would mean that the Bad Seeds would have to give up much of their self-reliance, at least for the time being, and would have to put up with the unfamiliar moods of an old hand. Indeed, the collaboration between Briggs and the musicians turned out to be extremely strenuous.

The first thing that struck the musicians was that Briggs was a strange old bird who had procedures that were quite unlike any of the band's own. Whereas Cave expressed his desire to retain all artistic control over the production, Briggs was totally unprepared to let anybody impinge on the way he thought things should be done. He wanted the songs recorded live and wasn't very fond of using subsequent overdubs. The producer had used this tactic to great advantage on some of Neil Young's legendary songs, such as 'Like a Hurricane', 'Cinnamon Girl', or 'My My, Hey Hey, (Out of the Blue)'. The way Briggs influenced the recordings was more of a spiritual nature than anything else: *'David was a kind of alchemist, he was solely interested in catching a magic moment; he knew exactly when it began and when it had run its course. He was the type of person that had been able to give Neil the opportunity to be the artist he was',* recalls Graham Nash, one of Neil Young's contemporaries. Great artists like Neil Young, The Grateful Dead, Bob Dylan, and most of the other American rock legends had frequently seen their world tours and album releases as expressions of work in progress rather than timeless statements. They had released several of their biggest albums with little fuss and rather unspectacularly, and working with professionals like Briggs had pushed them to tighten up their act and leave it to the producer to differentiate between moments of magic and ordinariness. As far as the Bad Seeds were concerned, this modus operandi led to a head-on collision with David Briggs during two recording sessions, one in New York's Dreamland Studios in November, the other in the Californian Sound City Studios in

December. Thomas Wydler still remembers with dread the band's collusion with Briggs: *'We had done some good work, but the songs sounded rubbish'.* The recordings didn't sound like the Bad Seeds, and, unlike 'From Her to Eternity', 'Kicking Against the Pricks' right up to 'The Good Son', showed none of the experimental vigour that had previously defined each and every Nick Cave album. The Bad Seeds' finished recordings had been cohesive, and were only rarely laid down on the spur of the moment. A particular track might have been comprised of several overdubs, and its homogenous sound was often the result of mixing various adaptations together. Just like Blixa Bargeld, who used to listen to his own band's latest recordings on Risiko's wonky cassette recorder before they were published, Nick Cave trusted in the sound of cheap stereo systems to let him see whether the underlying feel of his compositions came through. Like Wydler, he was disappointed when, for the first time, he heard the final versions of his new songs.

Hence, frustrated by the fruits of his labour, Nick spent Xmas 1991 back in Melbourne and decided to rework the tapes Briggs had delivered, in the New Year. Tony Cohen and Mick Harvey accompanied him into the city's Metropolis Studio and the three-man team produced a final cut that was more in alignment with Nick Cave's expectations. To their delight, the original raw recording now shone like a diamond. The album 'Henry's Dream' shows none of the difficulties the musicians had encountered recording it, thanks to the successful life-saving procedure Cave and Cohen had put it through. The nine tracks are pop music pure and continue the straightforward and direct openness of the album's predecessor. At the end of the day, Briggs's slave-driving technique had at least inspired the musicians to new heights. The songs, especially the single 'Jack The Ripper' and the two ballads 'Straight To You' and 'When I First Came To Town', are mesmerising and illustrate Cave's initial attempts to move into terrain that no longer had much in common with his underground roots. The nine perfectly timed and precisely arranged compositions are document to a new understanding of contemporary rock music, which, between the lines, infers: Nick Cave can try his hand at anything and do it well. The star photographer, Anton Corbijn, was hired to design the cover photo for the album in an attempt to match its musical step forward into the realms of controlled commercial success. This time, the cover was to be an illustration of Nick posing as a film star on a huge bill-board, and, perhaps due to the intoxicating quality of the album, fans and the music press received it without a word of criticism.

After its release in April 1992 'Henry's Dream' did much to establish Nick Cave as a dependable highly-acclaimed artist within the international independent music market, which was now worth millions. The serenity of the material allowed it to appeal to a broader audience, and Anton Corbijn was also commissioned to shoot the video for the single 'Straight To You'. The clip shows the Bad Seeds performing on the stage of a dank theatre. Each time they repeat the refrain, the curtain falls, and dancing girls, fire-eaters, and magicians fill in for the band until the next verse begins. Although the musicians later bemoaned the fact that filming was strenuous, as they had to change costumes and make-up a total of four times, the clip, in many ways reminiscent of the films of David Lynch, was the first Nick Cave video to meet MTV's stringent criteria —and not just those of the director who had shot it. No expense had been spared in shooting the video for the energy-laden rock song 'Jack The Ripper', produced by John Hillcoat, and, like its predecessor, the new clip was right up MTV's street. However, the channel did insist that the takes of fearsome, blood-smeared murder weapons on the video be removed before programmers were prepared to include it in the music station's schedules. Mute agreed and were over the moon when 'Henry's Dream' jumped to number 29 in the English charts.

The songs on 'Henry's Dream' are all accessible and document the new sense of composure that had been intrinsic in all of Cave's work since the release of 'The Good Son'. 'Straight To You' is a fatalistic song of love, its theme the pain of separation rather than the joys of passion. The singer mourns the passing of the romantic nights he had once enjoyed; now, all he has are memories: *'Gone are the nights from swinging from the stars.'* He pledges to return to his love, but his vow remains just that — a hollow promise to himself. If there is such a thing on 'Henry's Dream' as a common thread between the songs it contains, it is a definite sense of a homeland lost. In the song 'Papa Won't Leave You, Henry', the singer is on an Odyssey through a modern world that has lost its shine, he, at once sinner, whore-master, and too fond of his drink. He recalls the women he has known and loved, tells of the misery and injustice he has witnessed on his journey through life's harshness, and the indelible scars they have left in his mind. He sings of acts of revenge and abject poverty. *'Favelas exploding on inflammable spillways / Lynch-mobs, death squads, babies being born without brains.'* The only protection from the cruel world outside he can find is offered by the lullaby-like chorus of the song the narrator remembers his father singing to him when he was a boy. The lines that Cave sings are a reminder of happier days, a time when there was someone who wasn't afraid to show courage: *'Papa won't leave you, Henry / Papa won't leave you, boy / Well the road is long / And the road is hard / And many fall by the side / But Papa won't leave you, Henry / So there ain't no need to cry.'* The impact of grasping that life is full of sadness, with no hope of solace is the main tenet of the song – saudade. Cave alludes to endless sorrow in words that testify greatness: *'And all the tears we will weep today / Will be washed away / By the tears that we will weep tomorrow.'*

Like practically all the tracks on 'Henry's Dream', 'Papa Won't Leave You' is driven by the rhythms of an acoustic guitar, as is 'When I First Came to Town', an adaptation of the traditional American air 'Katy Cruel'. The original tear-jerker by Karen Dalton ('When I first came to town / They called me the roving jewel / Now they've changed their tune / They call me Katy Cruel') is one of the most moving laments ever sung. Nick Cave added several passages to the text and successfully transposed the mournful but proud basic mood of the original into a contemporary arrangement. In Cave's version, the singer sings of a journey without end. Wherever he settles, he is initially greeted with open arms: 'All the people gathered round / They bought me drinks.' But soon, these same people cast him out, and his journey continues. The words 'As though the blood on my hands / Is there for every citizen to see' infer that the song's protagonist is a murderer – and therefore an outlaw, his only certitude that in another city, 'A little further down the track', nothing will be different. Unlike all of Cave's previous work, this song is straight to the point and highly accessible. Conway Savage, the Bad Seeds' new pianist, accompanies Cave's insistent vocals, and a trio of strings, two violins and one cello, highlight the awful truth that the singer will have blood on his hands until the day he dies. 'Christina The Astonishing' again takes up the theme of restlessness, Cave accompanied solely by Mick Harvey's lamenting organ and Thomas Wydler's light percussion. Impressed by the story of Saint Christina of Liège from Albert Butler's 'The Lives of the Saints', first published in 1756, Nick took a bow before this Belgian figure of myth in his lyrics. Born in 1150, Christina was believed dead, and preparations had been made for her funeral. However, awoken from her apparent death by the smell of human sin, legend has it that she floated out of her open coffin. From then on, she attempted to avoid all further contact with people ('She fled to a remote place / Climbed towers and trees and walls / To escape the stench of human corruption.'), and died, aged 74, in the convent of St Catherine in Saint Trond. 'Christina The Astonishing' was to become an oasis of calm amidst the Bad Seeds's otherwise forceful live concerts and was played in the middle of every set for the next two years.

The lyrics on 'Henry's Dream' document that Nick Cave secretly felt troubled at spending much of his life on tour. They also illustrate his sadness at having no real home to call his own. However, Cave was starting to find some enjoyment in living the life of an itinerant expatriate and began to develop a new sense of purpose in his work, especially as the band's new line-up had resulted in a truly united front for the first time since Barry Adamson's resignation. Cave could hardly wait to set off on his longest tour yet. Twenty-four concerts were scheduled for April, May, and June throughout Europe, followed by 19 further performances in the US and Europe during the course of July, August, and September, and finally 17 shows in Australia and Japan in November, December, and January. Having to spend most of the year on the road to promote the album, the musicians, of course, had little opportunity to relax. Moreover, Die Haut were scheduled to give four individual performances in Vienna, Cologne, Hamburg and Berlin in August, and had invited Nick Cave along as a guest vocalist alongside other celebrities such as Kid Congo Powers, Anita Lane, Lydia Lunch, Alexander Hacke, and Blixa Bargeld. He jumped at the chance.

'Live At The Paradiso', the live footage shot by John Hillcoat on 2 and 3 July in Amsterdam, testifies to the maturity and vitality of the musicians' live performances in 1992. Their first live CD, 'Live Seeds', released in September, the only work to be published by the band that year, is equally impressive and contains twelve of their own compositions and one cover version, 'Plain Gold Ring', originally written by Earl S. Burroughs for Nina Simone. Simone released the track on her first album, 'Little Girl Blue', in 1957. She sings how the man she loves with all her heart has gone and married another women, the ring mentioned in the title the painful symbol of her desperation at never having the chance to be with him: 'In my heart it will never be spring / Long as he wears a plain gold ring'. Cave performed the song at an open-air concert in Melbourne in January 1993, and in his adaptation it takes on ominous overtones. Anybody who knows Cave's literary hunting grounds, even superficially, knows that Cave's rendering of the song was more than just a melancholy lament. The 'Live Seeds' CD was released with a short anthology of pictures shot by Melbourne photographer Peter Milne. One of them shows Nick Cave with a bag bearing the name of the Australian pop star Kylie Minogue. Cave had secretly hoped to record a duet with Kylie at some time in the future. However, in 1992, no-one could have guessed that this idée fixe would have tongues wagging.

The first time I met Nick was in New York in the early 80's. He was a lot of hair, grumpy, late and I was not at ease, actually mortified would be more precise. Nowadays he is not even late anymore and I always look forward to see him.

Anton Corbijn (1999)

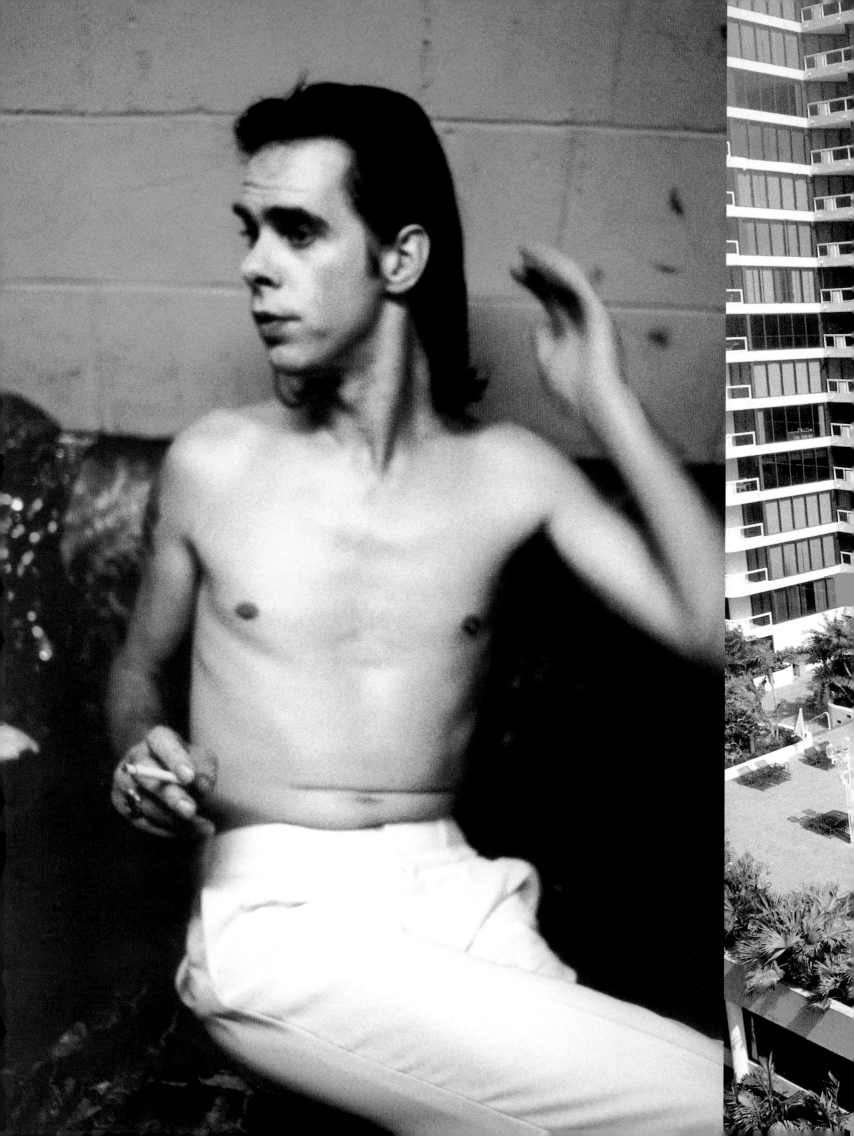

Amen

*Wanderer, wherever you go – at the end of your road death is
already waiting.*

Donald Duck

¹ And they came over unto the other side of the sea, into the
country of the Gad-a-renes'. ² And when he was come out of the
ship, immediately there met him out of the tombs a man with an
unclean spirit, ³ Who had his dwelling among the tombs; and no
man could bind him, no, not with chains: ⁴ Because that he had
been often bound with fetters and chains, and the chains had
been plucked asunder by him, and the fetters broken in pieces:
neither could any man tame him ⁵ And always, night and day, he
was in the mountains, and in the tombs, crying, and cutting himself with stones. ⁶ But when he saw Jesus afar off, he ran and
worshipped him, ⁷ And cried with a loud voice, and said, What
have I to do with thee, Jesus, thou Son of the most high God?
I adjure thee by God, that thou torment me not. ⁸ For he said unto
him, Come out of the man, thou unclean spirit. ⁹ And he asked
him, What is thy name? And he answered, saying, My name is
Legion: for we are many. ¹⁰ And he besought him much that he
would not send them away out of the country. ¹¹ Now there was
there nigh unto the mountains a great herd of swine feeding.
¹² And all the devils besought him, saying, Send us into the swine,
that we may enter into them. ¹³ And forth with Jesus gave them
leave. And the unclean spirits went out, and entered into the
swine: and the herd ran violently down a steep place into the sea,
(they were about two thousand;) and were choked in the sea.
¹⁴ And they that fed the swine fled, and told it in the city, and in
the country. And they went out to see what it was that was done.
¹⁵ And they come to Jesus, and see him that was possessed with
the devil, and had the legion, sitting, and clothed, and in his right

mind: and they were afraid. [16] And they that saw it told them how it befell to him that was possessed with the devil, and also concerning the swine. [17] And they began to pray him to depart out of their coasts. [18] And when he was come into the ship, he that had been possessed with the devil prayed him that he might be with him. [19] Howbeit Jesus suffered him not, but saith unto him, Go home to thy friends, and tell them how great things the Lord hath done for thee, and hath had compassion on thee. [20] And he departed, and began to publish in De-cap'-o-lis how great things Jesus had done for him: and all men did marvel. *[Mark 5 / 1-20]*

In 1998 Nick Cave was invited to take part in an unusual literary project organised by the reputable Scottish publishing house Canongate Books Ltd. As one of a selected few publishers with the right to print copies of the Authorised Version of the King James Bible, Canongate came up with the idea of bringing out affordable individual paperback versions of the bible's various books. The reasoning behind this was the evidence that fewer and fewer people were still truly interested in the teachings of what they saw as a dogmatic and increasingly alienated church doctrine. The publisher's prime intention was to alleviate people's misgivings about combing through hundreds of pages of small print by providing potential readers with a much more inviting bible format. Canongate's 'Pocket Canons' stuck to the numeration of the traditional verses of the King James while attempting to present them as complete works in their own right, thus reflecting the original shape of the books prior to their inclusion in the bible. The publishers approached them as works of literature, at the same time transposing them into a contemporary context discretely designed to appeal to present-day readers. Celebrities in the field of literature such as Doris Lessing, Will Self, and Nick Cave were invited by Canongate to write the forewords to each edition, prefaces that would interpret the books from a personal non-theological standpoint in a thoroughly indiscriminate and non-intrusive way. Nick Cave was among the initial twelve authors Canongate approached, and he was given the choice of writing the introduction to either Genesis, Exodus, Job, Ecclesiastes, Proverbs, The Song of Solomon, Corinthians, Revelation, or one of the four gospels of Matthew, Mark, Luke, and John. Nick Cave opted for the Gospel according to Mark which tells the story of the life and resurrection of Jesus Christ in a more forthright, fast-moving and direct manner than any of the other three.

In his introduction, Nick Cave outed himself as a believer. As a young man, the singer wrote in his essay, the Old Testament with its scenes of brutality and harshness had captivated him. Cave had also been thoroughly taken by the idea of a vengeful god who forever tried his eternally suffering children by bringing down upon them one horrific catastrophe after another. This was a deity who was an omnipresent symbol of the underlying iniquity of human-

kind as well as an attestation to the fact that evil was a tangible force that could befall anyone at any time. Cave wrote of his perception of the bible: *'Evil seemed to live so close to the surface of existence (…), you could smell its mad breath, see the yellow smoke curl from its many pages, hear the bloodcurdling moans of despair.'* The Australian believes the Old Testament is both magnificent and desolate, but as he grew older, the castigating Judge of humankind who so steadfastly upheld the principle of vengeance – an eye for an eye, a tooth for a tooth – slowly started to lose much of His former profundity and allure. Nick Cave still considers himself a Christian but no longer adheres to the belief in an omnipotent meddling Godhead, preferring instead the idea that life on earth may have a deeper meaning to which the bible may hold the key. Having avoided it like the plague for thirty years, Cave only turned to the New Testament later in life, although he had been raised as an Anglican and had even sung in the church choir in Wangaratta as a young boy – *'I recall thinking what a wishy-washy affair the whole thing was.'*

Three decades later Nick Cave, like many other adults who have read the Gospels for the first time, was surprised at how short the texts were. Theologians agree that Mark is the most ancient of the four Gospels. It was originally passed from generation to generation by word of mouth and describes the life of Christ in small episodes that were propagated by teachers and prophets. The Gospel according to Mark is defined by a simple linguistic beauty and is a breathtaking narrative of a succession of events, sermons, commandments, and parables, all of which form the general consensus of Western civilisation. Nick Cave was struck by the enormous stylistic power that inspires the euphoric narration of the story. He writes: *'Mark's gospel is a clatter of bones, so raw, nervy and lean on information that the narrative aches with the melancholy of absence.'* While he was busying himself with biblical themes, Cave began to detect a fatalistic kind of humour in the Holy Scriptures. *'The greatest isolation Christ had to endure',* Cave writes, *'wasn't the forty days and forty nights he spent in the desert (where Jesus had resisted the temptations of Satan), but the humiliation of being misunderstood by his twelve disciples.'* The story is familiar: the Son of God performs miracles in Israel and preaches the doctrine of love thy neighbour. However, his repeated calls for discretion on the part of those whom he has healed of disease and faithlessness fall on deaf ears. The healed tell the Pharisees, upholders of the old paradigm, all about the wondrous talents of the Son of God. The Pharisees subsequently denounce Jesus as a charlatan and begin their persecution of the Messiah. The rest, as they say, is history. Nick Cave's perception of faith is explained in his preface to Mark: *'Christ spoke to me through his isolation, through the burden of his premature death, through his anger at the material world, through his pain.'* The singer describes the Saviour as the victim of an ignorant society, devoid of foresight and imagination which treats those who are different with barbaric cruelty. In Mark's Gospel, Cave uncovered a view of Christ totally distinct from the one usually put across by the church. Jesus appears more adept, witty and courageous than the people around Him. *'Christ understood that we as humans were forever held to the ground by the pull of gravity – our ordinariness, our mediocrity – and it was through His example that He gave our imaginations the freedom to rise and to fly. In short, to be Christ-like.'*

When 'The Boatman's Call', the tenth studio album by Nick Cave and the Bad Seeds, was released in 1997, a year prior to the book project, Cave had already given to the world his opinions on religion during interviews with the media. He told Hamburg journalist Christoph Twickel: *'The life of Christ as told in the bible seems to me to be an encrypted, powerful story, practically a metaphor for all the tribulations humans must suffer. I believe the message of Christ is that we must shake off all those demons that stop us from reaching our potential as human beings.'* The majority of reporters were interested in the singer's spiritual well-being, mainly because the cycle of songs on 'The Boatman's Call' is a twelve-fold treatise on the typically human quest for meaning, love and fulfilment. The songs saw Nick Cave cast off the protective shielding that the Bad Seeds had provided over the years, and 'The Boatman's Call' was an obvious and authentic solo album, the band merely the accompaniment. The singer had looked within himself and now started to regard the world and his relationship to women in a more introspective light. The songs on the album reflect the duality of Cave's Weltanschauung – no pain without consolation, no joy without sorrow – and he discovered a role for himself in his distillation of a man who had known suffering for most of his life. The songs are basic, deliberate and intimate in the way Cave tackles them, and his minimal piano arrangements do much to enhance this sparseness. The opening track, 'Into My Arms', leaves no doubt to the direction Cave intended to take on his final album release of the millennium. *'I don't believe in an interventionist god'* is the first line of the track and therefore the opening line of the album and is directed towards a woman: *'But if I did, I would kneel down and ask Him / Not to intervene when it came to you / Not to touch a hair on your head / To leave you as you are / And if He felt He had to direct you / Then direct you into my arms.'* However, the love songs on 'The Boatman's Call' also have their darker sides. Any praises sung to the beloved are followed by bitter recriminations and remarks that leave love unfulfilled. In '(Are You) The One I've Been Waiting For' the singer meditates on the love in his heart as he sings: *'My soul has comforted and assured me / That in time my heart it will reward me / And that all will be revealed.'* Two short verses later Cave curbs his excruciating passion, looks up to the night sky and ascertains: *'The stars will explode in the sky / O but they don't, do they? / Stars have their moment and then they die.'*

The Australian sees the world from askance on 'The Boatman's Call'. He explained the reason for his belated discovery of the New Testament as being the calming influence of time, and now that he had grown older, he had started to forgive himself and others for their mistakes instead of seeking hot-headed confrontation. In earlier masterpieces such as 'Mutiny in Heaven', heaven and hell had been the bizarre settings for bloodthirsty burlesques, and the dead, mutilated and desperate had been dotted all over the place. 'Idiot Prayer', conversely, describes heaven and hell as philosophical concepts. The poet dispatches a carrier pigeon bearing a message of farewell to his mistress, hoping he will meet her again in heaven. However, Cave inserted a few lines which give the ballad a hidden sarcastic note. *'If you're in Heaven then you'll forgive me, dear / Because that's what they do up there / But if you're in Hell, then what can I say / You probably deserved it anyway.'* In 1998 and 1999 Nick Cave gave two readings: 'The love song – and how to write it', at the Akademie der Künste in Vienna and 'The secret life of the love song' in London's Royal Festival Hall. He put forward that a love song must also contain moments of grief and loneliness. Love songs that only show passion sunny-side-up are, in fact, well camouflaged hate songs, according to Cave who went on to record 'Far From Me', the most beautiful song on 'The Boatman's Call', to prove his theory. The singer laments the woman he loves who left him many moons ago, and in singing her praises, feels the pain of her absence like little needles that pierce his heart: *'Through the thick and through the thin / Those were your very words / My fair-weather friend / You were my brave-hearted lover / At the first taste of trouble went running back to mother.'* The Bad Seeds, who had recorded 'The Boatman's Call' with Nick Cave in 1996, now consisted of seven members after having been joined by Jim Sclavunos, formerly of Sonic Youth from New York, on percussion, and Warren Ellis, violinist with the Australian band The Dirty Three. These newcomers greatly enriched the band's sound, especially Ellis, whose violin fitted in perfectly with their musical concept. It is interesting to note that the Bad Seeds' new potential big-band sound ironically led to their recording the most musically frugal and introverted of any of Cave's albums.

Four years earlier, 1993 had been the year in which the wheel of fortune had started to pick up speed and, from then on, would never slow down. Nick Cave and the Bad Seeds were caught in a maelstrom of events that would symbolise their routine until 1996. During this time life was almost exclusivlely dictated by a succession of tours and studio sessions. The Bad Seeds had stayed on in mainland Europe and Australia after Nick had returned to London from São Paolo in 1993, so the thousands of miles between them still meant that the band only got together with their lead singer whenever there was work to be done. As each of the band members was involved with other groups or working on

individual projects, such as producing, writing soundtracks, or solo recordings, nearly every month that passed brought another record release by a current or former member of Nick Cave's band. These were often inspired works but seldom attained the uniqueness Cave's vocals bestowed on the Bad Seeds, with a few notable exceptions: Die Einstürzenden Neubauten were a hard-working band who, back in 1989, had recorded a modern rock classic with their album 'Haus der Lüge'. In 1993 Anita Lane's album 'Dirty Pearl' created a singular blend of scepticism and pride, which, to this day, can be ranked as one of the most excellent recordings to be made by an artist from the Bad Seeds' circle. Barry Adamson's six-track mini album 'The Negro Inside Me', also released in 1993, has lost none of its shine since, and his mostly instrumental songs are magnificent. Due to the busy time schedules of the individual members, any meeting of the Bad Seeds required considerable logistical planning.

Nick Cave and the Bad Seeds' 1994 release, 'Let Love In', proved that they could sustain an even greater mood of achievement than they had established after the commercial success of 'Henry's Dream'. Flanked by 'Do You Love Me?', the band's best-selling single up till then, 'Let Love In' jumped to no. 12 in the English charts, thus assuring that the 77 concerts scheduled for the musicians' busy tour of Europe sold out and that they were placed third on the bill of the American Lollapalooza Festival stadium tour. With 'Let Love In' Cave and the band finally emerged from the familiar underground of the business and planted themselves firmly in the shark-infested overground scene. They managed to survive unscathed. The new, easily accessible album had successfully allowed the musicians to take control of their own marketability, and Nick Cave and Mick Harvey both described this as the most momentous and significant step the band had ever taken during their ten years together. 'Let Love In' is the essence of the unmistakable sound the band had developed over the past few years on their albums. The ten songs were more memorable than ever before and were thus prepared for a market that sees music as a commodity, an image as packaging, and an artist as a trademark. In playing the game Cave had recorded an album that didn't resist the laws of the market, but he was in a position to retain full artistic control over it. The Bad Seeds had availed themselves of a variety of styles, oscillating between the extremes of vaudeville and bar music, rock and country, to come up with a musical framework on which Nick Cave could lay out his surprisingly personal lyrics. Nick had written several of the songs about the devastating relationship he had had with Viviane Carneiro. His verses testify to a profound sense of self-accusation, confession, and reconciliation, and, like many singers before him, Nick was expressing the feelings that plagued him through his songs. The album vacillates between admonishment and the pleasures of being in love, and, for the first time, Cave is singing in the first person instead of hiding behind some imaginary character, as he was prone to do in the past. 'Do You Love Me? (Part 2)', the final track on the album, is the one that shines brightest. Its chamber music-like arrangement and its gentle strings tell the pitiful tale of a small boy who is enticed into a cinema and seduced by a man *'with sly girlish eyes'*. Instead of using the song to deplore what has unfolded, although he would certainly be right in doing so, Cave prefers to remain objective and puts forward the intricate question whether this (involuntary) first sexual encounter will render impossible a second more innocent experience, as the boy may never again be able to experience love without preconceptions. In the cinema, the boy naively asks *'Do you love me?'*, the man with the girlish eyes replying: *'Yes, I love you, you are handsome'*. This is the question lovers typically ask, but here the issue remains unresolved as to whether the boy, after this defining incident in a dark movie theatre, will ever be able to combine love and sex with all the positive connotations they normally imply. The song finishes with the lines: *'Memories that become monstrous lies / So onward! And Onward I go / Onward! And Upward! And I'm off to find love / With blue-black bracelets on my wrists and ankles / And the coins in my pocket go jingle jangle.'* 'Do You Love Me? (Part 2)' is an epic portrayed in a similar vein to the final scene in a cheerless film. Again, the song's inherent message is: there is no cure for sorrow, as the vast majority of Cave's earlier works allude to. Fans saw in Nick Cave a modern-day sufferer, a rare valiant character of feeling who refused to sacrifice himself to the rationality of a post-industrial world. Hence his personal insights as expressed in his songs hit the nerve. The dynamic 'Let Love In' has often been described as Cave's best album. In fact, the album comes across as being so 'perfect', because it was the first album of the underground hero to be presented in perfect stereo, an attribute that the majority of people would not normally have ascribed to him. The individual songs on 'Let Love In' sound faultless simply because they are like more refined versions of material the band had already released as blueprints on earlier albums. Nick Cave, the critics decreed, had come up with the goods and presented the world with an album that was devoid of abrupt style changes or painful omissions. But there were also discordant voices who accused the singer of having gone too mainstream by giving into audience demands, but they were drowned out by the volume of the Bad Seeds' music.

Now that Nick Cave's albums were selling in droves, he now guaranteed Mute Records a steady source of income, although to a lesser extent than Depeche Mode and Erasure. In 1995, Mute therefore had no reservations about giving the Australian a free reign. After several tours and a moderately successful duet with his friend Shane MacGowan of The Pogues (an agreeable cover of the Louis Armstrong evergreen 'What a Wonderful World') Cave accepted a number of independent commissions, such as

WHAT SORT OF MAN READS HUSTLER?

He has a thirst for life's pleasures. Fiercely individualistic, he commands a group setting with intoxicating dexterity. Nick Cave has guided his band of musical malcontents, the Bad Seeds, through 12 years and nine albums of outlaw rock 'n' roll—and he's read HUSTLER every step of the way. Five out of five HUSTLER readers prefer sexy, dangerous diversions, such as *Murder Ballads*, the latest collection of killer songs by Nick Cave and the Bad Seeds (on Mute/Reprise Records). HUSTLER men also prefer being surrounded by naked chicks. That's why Nick Cave toasts America's Magazine. (Source: August 1996 LFP.)

an uplifting contribution to the Hollywood blockbuster 'Batman Forever'. Now free to turn his mind to other projects, Cave was gripped by a strong desire to record a duet with the Australian teen idol Kylie Minogue for a concept album he was planning, entitled 'Murder Ballads'. 'Where The Wild Roses Grow' was the only Nick Cave hit to reach the top ten almost in every country of the world, as hordes of Kylie fans went out and bought the single in addition to Nick's army of admirers.

The recipe was brilliant in its simplicity. Cave had condensed his long-time preoccupation with death and killings into a wholesome formula in 'Where The Wild Roses Grow'. Cave divided the roles much akin to a fairytale, 'Beauty And The Beast' a perfect analogy. It takes the form of an exchange between Cave, a murderer who, in the real world, had a sinister image that was difficult to fathom, and his victim, Kylie, in 1995 the embodiment of innocence and light. The ideal ingredients for a chart stormer. Nick had long since learned to deal with pop symbols and codes intuitively and had now unexpectedly turned into an expert manipulator in a hugely intricate media show. The video contributed much to the song's success with its visualisation of the incredible – the murder of Australia's national treasure, Kylie Minogue, by its most controversial rock star. The clip had been shot with MTV's stringent criteria obviously in mind, both ironic and slick with its allure of a cool advertising trailer. MTV included the video in their heavy rotation schedule, broadcasting 'Where The Wild Roses Grow' several times a day over a period of several months during 1996. The scandal caused by Kylie's role as a pretty, soaking corpse was conjured up more or less on purpose. The clip's apparent romanticising of murdering women resulted in Australian broadcasters even going as far as to call for a boycott of both song and singers. Furthermore, many of Cave's fans who had happily gone along with 'Let Love In' felt let down by his apparent willingness to be seduced by the piles of money and the commercial success the duet with Kylie promised. In fans' eyes, Cave should never have stooped that low. Nick had never made a secret of his admiration for Kylie Minogue and was himself a fan of the mass-appeal popsongs that Stock, Aitken, and Waterman had produced for the former soap icon. Kylie's image may have been trivial and trite, but at least it was authentic. Cave's own preoccupation with murderers, psychopaths and religion had often been trivial at its core as well, but the poet had always been able to transform the triteness of his songs into a dramatic manifestation and had constantly portrayed deep-seated emotions or even irrefutable truths in them. Kylie's hit single 'Better The Devil You Know' with its simple but poetic lyrics had inspired Cave to write the duet for her when he had first come across it several years before.

'Murder Ballads', Cave's ninth album, is a showpiece. The concept behind it enabled him to take his skeletons out of the cupboard and exorcise his demons, psychological baggage that had accompanied Cave on his every move towards the limits of human endurance. Casting out demons is a main element in Mark's Gospel, although Cave had partly brought forth his particular set himself. The Australian decided to leave his interest in inherently violent and dangerous psychopaths behind him once the album was released to concentrate more on love and religious contemplations. 'Murder Ballads' is as bloodthirsty as its title implies. There are 66 corpses on the album, murdered by seven men and three women, one of Cave's victims an unfortunate terrier that has been nailed to a door. Cave's sleeves-up exaggerated preoccupation with crimes of passion, vulnerability or badness has such a large streak of black humour running straight through it that the fates the songs describe provoke little reaction – quite unlike those in previous works in which Cave had dedicated himself to his favourite topic with gusto. The tales the ballads divulge are therefore more akin to grotesque, brutal children's songs, such as those of Wilhelm Busch, except that Cave only moralises in one of them, preferring instead to describe the course of events in a more gentle and romantic technique. The singer had ensured that the album's stringent concept was strictly adhered to, as he justifiably had been worried that the songs on 'Let Love In' might define the final step on his long journey, especially in their over exaggeration of familiar motifs and Cave's typical musical style. For the first time ever, the 37 year-old singer had been in a position to work on the album with a sense of greater emotional detachment. After its release in 1996, Cave said of 'Murder Ballads' that it was a form of literary expression without precedent in any of his former works. It delved into the art of storytelling – art for art's sake. Murder ballads belong to the musical traditions of every culture and every language has its songs about murderers and their dastardly deeds alongside the lullabies, love songs, drinking airs, and kitchen rhymes. In days gone by, songs served the same purpose as fairytales, poems were messages that were passed down from generation to generation, poetic documents of rules and proscriptions. An offshoot of the Sicilian Cosa Nostra, the Calabrian 'Ndranghetà, even kept record of the actions, martyrdoms, and laws of their secret institution – from the beginning of the century, when it was founded, right up to the 1970s – in melancholy laments and convicts' songs, as they had to be careful that there was no written evidence to incriminate them. Cave's murder ballads therefore are oriented towards songs that had already been written, which goes some way to explain why the album is so composed and makes no allusion to contemporary trends. 'Murder Ballads' was an étude by an artist who had realised that he was at a crossroads for the umpteenth time, grasped that he wanted to break with the past, but didn't yet know which road to follow. In hindsight, releasing an album to which he had no great attachment and which had turned into his biggest commercial success was the best thing that could ever have happened to a performer who had come so far.

By 1997 Cave had arrived and was able to slow down and catch his breath. 'The Boatman's Call' proved that he had mastered the feelings of helplessness that had been reflected on his two hugely successful albums, 'Let Love In' and 'Murder Ballads'. Cave now took to repositioning himself and his music after having stormed the charts in 1996 and subsequently releasing his most serious and mature album of his career one year later. It certainly appeared that he had reached all of his goals. The singer also had time to dedicate himself to all those things he would never have dared to approach in the past for fear of being misunderstood. Cave's status was now that of a major player in the international cultural circus. Whenever he played the piano, for example as he did at one of the rare public showings of Carl Dreyer's 1928 silent movie classic 'La passion de Jeanne d'Arc' at a special screening in a London cinema, the media sat up and took note. A celebrity like Nick Cave may also profit from the fact that public institutions and private organisations are frequently keen to be linked to a famous name to enhance their image. The Schauspielhaus in Düsseldorf approached him in 1997 with the idea of his composing the accompanying music for a one-off showing of Fritz Lang's 'Metropolis', although time constraints meant that he had to decline. Nick did, however, find time in June 1999 to become the patron of the prestigious Meltdown Festival in London, where he surprised his fans with an unexpected but highly visual reckoning with his past. In booking Alan Vega (Suicide), Lee Hazlewood, and Nina Simone, he brought together three of the main influences on his musical career. He made use of the free hand the organisers of the festival had given him to invite artists on board as diverse as the Estonian minimalist Avo Pärt, the Polish composer Lech Janovski, the Australian comedian Barry Humphries (aka Dame Edna), as well as his mates from The Dirty Three, giving them all an excellent opportunity to join forces and play in front of a large audience. Nick had even tried to get Bob Dylan, Johnny Cash, and John Lee Hooker to appear on the same night, but time constraints put an end to that idea. Prior to and after the Meltdown Festival Cave appeared at various prestigious European jazz festivals, accompanied by three unpretentious musicians including Warren Ellis from The Dirty Three, and played the piano himself. This experiment in music without the familiar company of the Bad Seeds saw Nick Cave depart on a new quest. He was back on the path that had brought him his greatest – and his most modest – triumphs, withstanding the temptation to recycle the success 'Where The Wild Roses Grow' had ensured.

The Russian poet Fyodor Dostoevsky included a quotation from the Gospel of John in the preface to 'The Brothers Karamazov'. *'Verily, verily, I say unto you, Except a corn of wheat fall into the ground and die, it abideth alone: but if it die, it bringeth forth much fruit.'* In his epic story of patricide, the Russian uses the orphaned sons, of which there are three, and their differing views on their

homeland, society, and God to deliver his final statement of faith shortly before his own death. Alyosha, the youngest brother, studies the Word of God in a monastery where the Scriptures are interpreted in a manner supportive of humankind. He feels a profound sense of attachment to his Russian soul while his brother, Dimitri, the eldest of the three, full of the passion of a free-thinking but destitute liver of life. Finally, Ivan is an intellectual sceptic who cannot come to terms with God, choosing to believe in a utopia that has still to be established, *'everything is permissible'* his basis for denying faith. Dostoevsky started his novel with the metaphor of a grain of wheat, because the cycle of renewal also represents the cycle of mankind, of life and of creative expression. Dostoevsky dedicated his epilogue to children and hence to hope. He ascertains that children are born innocent and only lose themselves in the mists of confusion as they progress on their passage to adulthood, some of their minds corrupted on this tortuous journey. Dostoevsky died in 1881 shortly after he had completed his two-volume epic, unable to fulfil his last goal in life. He had intended to write a short, more optimistic book to follow 'The Brothers Karamazov', a Russian variation of Voltaire's 'Candide' which, in the original, bears the subtitle 'The Best Of All Worlds'. Dostoevsky's literary testament implores us all to assume the guilt of the world in order to purify our souls. Dostoevsky: *'There is only one ultimate ideal on Earth – the concept of the immortality of the human soul, because upholding any other fundamental idea which may nourish the human spirit has its sole source there ... In short, immortality is life itself, existence its principle purpose.'*

In the late summer of 1999, Nick Cave married his girlfriend, Susie Bick. He now lives with his wife, children and cats on a boat somewhere in England.

I wish I would have never met this man.

Anita Lane (1999)

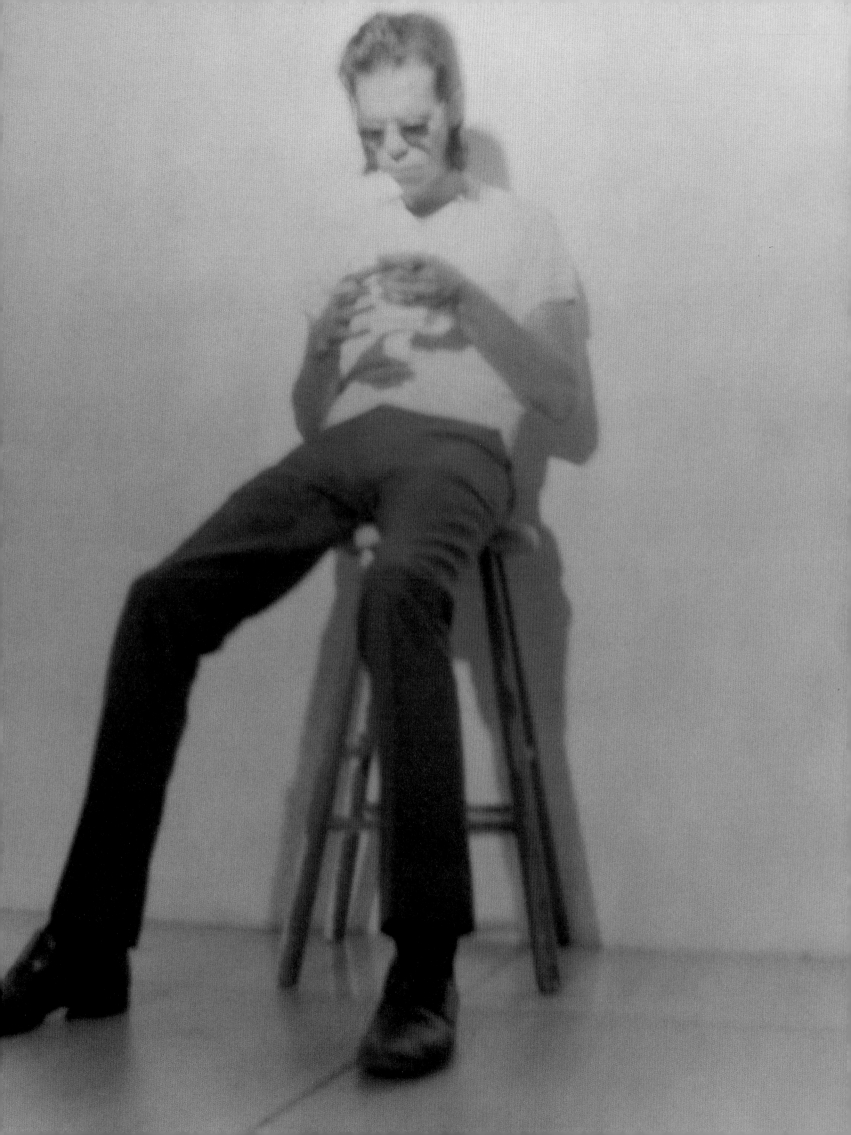

Cover: Nick Cave at the grand piano at the Holiday Inn, Munich, © 1997 Johannes Beck, Berlin

Page **6**: Nick Cave in Hyde Park, London. Photo production commissioned by Wire Magazine. © 1999 Frank Bauer, London

Page **7**: Nicholas Edward Cave age 2 1/2, © 1960 Dawn Cave, Melbourne. Cave family album. Reproduction with kind permission of Dawn Cave.

Page **8 / 9**: The Class of 1970 at Caulfield Grammar (Nick seated in first row, 8th from left), © 1970 unknown, Cave family album.

Page **10**: Nicholas Edward Cave age 14, © 1972 Dawn Cave, Melbourne. Cave family album. Reproduction with kind permission of Dawn Cave.

Page **11**: Nicholas Edward Cave age 19, © 1977 Dawn Cave, Melbourne. Cave family album. Reproduction with kind permission of Dawn Cave.

Page **12 / 13**: Cave family residence in Melbourne Garden City, © 1985 Elisabeth Krause, Sontra

Page **18**: '2 Cute Cunts', Collage, © 1985 Nick Cave, archives minus publishing, Berlin

Page **20 / 21**: The Boys Next Door in Nick's room at home (left to right: Mick Harvey, Phill Calvert, Rowland S. Howard, Tracy Pew, Nick Cave), © 1984 Peter Milne, Melbourne

Page **22**: Anita Lane age 17, © 1977 Ann Wilson (?), Melbourne. Photo privately owned by Anita Lane.

Page **23**: Nick Cave in a fish'n'chip shop in Melbourne, © 1977 Genevieve McGuckin (?), Melbourne, Photo privately owned by Anita Lane, herself in the background.

Page **24 / 25**: Portrait of The Boys Next Door (from left to right: Tracy Pew, Nick Cave, Mick Harvey, Phill Calvert), © 1977 Peter Milne, Melbourne. Photo procured from the Australian Cave Archives est. by Andrew and Lynne Trute, Melbourne

Page **26**: Tracy Pew and Mick Harvey during a Boys Next Door gig on January 1 1980 at the Bottom Line Club, Royal Oak Hotel in Melbourne's Richmond district, © 1980 Jeff Busby, Melbourne

Page **27**: Nick Cave live in Melbourne during a Boys Next Door gig in 1979, © 1979 probably by Bruno Adams, Photo procured from the Australian Cave Archives est. by Andrew and Lynne Trute, Melbourne

Page **28**: The Boys Next Door on 24.4.1979, Crystal Ballroom, Melbourne, © 1979 Jeff Busby, Melbourne

The Visuals

Page **29**: The Boys Next Door on 24.4.1979 live at the Crystal Ballroom, Melbourne. Left front: clear view of the chandelier that gave the venue its name, © 1979 Jeff Busby, Melbourne

Page **30 / 31**: Deserted London tube station, © 1981 Nicholas Seferi, Melbourne

Page **36**: Three pictures from a Birthday Party photo session, © 1981 Peter Milne, Melbourne

Page **38**: Nick Cave smoking, with a crucifix and styled hair-do in London 1982, © 1982 Andrew Catlin, London

Page **40**: Lydia Lunch in a pond near Berlin, © 1982 Peter Gruchot, Berlin

Page **41**: Nick Cave during a gig with The Birthday Party at the Hammersmith Palace in London, © 1982 Andrew Catlin, London

Page **42 / 43**: Nick Cave live at the Zig-Zag Club in London, © 1982 Andrew Catlin, London

Page **44 / 45**: Nick Cave on stage of The Hammersmith Palace in London sometime in the early eighties, © 198-(?), Andrew Catlin, London

Page **46 / 47**: Nick Cave with 'Porco Dio' (sic) on his breast in the video for 'Nick The Stripper', © 1981 Directed by: Paul Goldman, D.O.P Evan English, Production: Lucy MacLaren, Cut: David Biltmore

Page **48 / 49**: SO 36 in Berlin after a concert, © 1982 Anno Dittmer, Berlin

Page **55**: Blixa Bargeld at the premiere of '1/2 Mensch' by Shogo Ishii at the Arsenal cinema, Berlin, © 1986 Petra Gall, Berlin

Page **57**: Nick Cave in a red suit during a gig in April 1986 in Melbourne, © 1986 Ross Waterman, Melbourne

Page **58**: Nick Cave at his desk, at home in Melbourne, © 1985 Elisabeth Krause, Sontra

Page **59**: Nick Cave in his mother's garden in Melbourne, © 1985 Elisabeth Krause, Sontra

Page **60 / 61**: The Birthday Party at their last concert with Mick Harvey at The Electric Ballroom on April 26, 1983, © 1983 Andrew Catlin, London

Page **62**: Nick Cave smoking during a concert at the Bains Douches in Paris in June 1982, © 1982 Andrew Catlin, London

Page **63**: Nick Cave noticeably exhausted during a concert on March 27 1982 in the Warehouse in Liverpool, © 1982 Andrew Catlin, London

Page **64 / 65**: Morning view of Yorckstrasse through the railings of Risiko bar in Berlin. From 'Lost', a court metrage by Uli M. Schüppel, about the last night of Risiko on 30.4.1986, © 1986 Uli M. Schüppel, Berlin

Page **68**: Text and photo collage, © 1987 Nick Cave, archives minus publishing, Berlin

Page **70**: Nick Cave at a desk in his room in Dresdner Strasse in Berlin (Still from the film 'Dandy' by Peter Sempel), © 1986 Peter Sempel, Hamburg

Page **74**: Nick Cave and Anita Lane in the visitors' crash-out area in Christoph Dreher's loft in Dresdner Strasse in Berlin, © 1984 Rainer Berson, Wien

Page **75** (top): Rowland S. Howard in bed with Nick Cave, © 1984 Rainer Berson, Wien

Seite **75** (bottom): Nick Cave and Blixa Bargeld during one of their first encounters in the lift at Hansa-Studio, Berlin, © 1984 Peter Gruchot, Berlin

Page **76**: Nick Cave in Oranienstrasse in Berlin-Kreuzberg, © 1984 Elisabeth Krause, Sontra

Page **77**: Portrait of Nick Cave, © 1986 Petra Gall, Berlin

Page **78 / 79**: Nick Cave and Blixa Bargeld during a concert on 30.9.1986 at the Tempodrom, Berlin, © 1986 Petra Gall, Berlin

Page **80**: Portrait of Nick Cave, © 1986 Peter Gruchot, Berlin

Page **81** (top): Nick Cave with sunglasses looking out a car window in Yorckstrasse, Berlin (Still from the film 'Dandy' by Peter Sempel), © 1986 Peter Sempel, Hamburg

Page **81** (bottom): Maria Zastrow (aka Don Elvis) behind the bar at Risiko, © 1984 Petra Gall, Berlin

Page **82 / 83**: Nick Cave's exceedingly toe-pinching right shoe on top of a monitor speaker during a concert in London Hammersmith Palace in 1985, © 1985 Andrew Catlin, London

Page **88**: Nick Cave kneeling on stage of The Mean Fiddler in London on October 14, 1986 (?), © 1986 Andrew Catlin, London

Page **89**: 'Elvis Cunt Back', sketch, © 1985 Nick Cave, archives minus publishing, Berlin

Page **93**: Excerpt from a concert announcement for a club in Madrid, © 1984 unknown, from the private collection of Beate Bartel, Berlin

Page **94 / 95**: Band portrait of the Bad Seeds at the Hansa-Studio, Berlin (left to right: Barry Adamson, Nick Cave, Mick Harvey, Blixa Bargeld), © 1984 Jutta Henglein, Berlin

Page **96** (top): Nick Cave in Times Square, New York, © 1992 Peter Sempel, Hamburg

Page **96** (bottom): Blixa Bargeld and Mick Harvey in front of a wall pasted with posters in Florence, © 1984 Beate Bartel, Berlin

Page **97**: Nick Cave at a desk at his mother's place, © 1985, Elisabeth Krause, Sontra

Page **98 / 99** : Nick Cave smoking during a Bad Seeds concert at The Electric Ballroom in London in 1984 (?), © 1984, Andrew Catlin, London

Page **100 / 101**: Nick Cave on stage of The Hammersmith Palace in London sometime in 1985, © 1985 Andrew Catlin, London

Page **102 / 103**: Bad Seeds audience in The Hammersmith Palace in London sometime in 1985, © 1985 Andrew Catlin, London

Page **104 / 105**: Suite at the Mariott Hotel in Miami, Florida on 15.8.1994, © 1994 Kai Reinhardt, Dortmund

Page **108**: Illustration, © 1985 Nick Cave. From a letter from Nick to Elisabeth. With kind permission of Elisabeth Krause, Sontra

Page **114 / 115** (top left): Nick Cave and Brad Pitt in 'Johnny Suede', Regie: Tom DiCillo, © 1991 Tom DiCillo, New York. Photo: courtesy of Tom DiCillo.

Page **115** (top right): Scene from the documentary 'The Road To God Knows Where' by Uli M. Schüppel, (left to right: Mick Harvey, Nick Cave, Roland Wolf, Thomas Wydler, Kid Congo Powers), © 1989 Uli M. Schüppel, Berlin

Page **114 / 115** (bottom left): Nick Cave at the Große Freiheit 36, Hamburg © 1992, Stefan Malzkorn, Hamburg

Page **115** (bottom right): Nick Cave in a scene from the motion picture 'Ghosts … Of The Civil Dead' (Australia 1988), © 1988 Evan English / John Hillcoat, London

Page **116**: Nick Cave with guitar and chewing gum cigarette, © 1985 Elisabeth Krause, Sontra

Page **117** (top left): Nick Cave with his mother, Dawn, in Melbourne, © 1985 Elisabeth Krause, Sontra

Page **117** (top right): Nick Cave and Elisabeth Recker in front of their caravan, © 1985 Elisabeth Krause, Sontra

Page **117** (bottom left): Nick Cave toasting the bride, © 1985 Elisabeth Krause, Sontra

Page **117** (bottom right): Nick Cave, John Hillcoat and a stranger in Melbourne, © 1985 Elisabeth Krause, Sontra

Page **118**: The Bad Seeds live in Melbourne, © 1990 Beate Bartels, Berlin

Page **119**: Nick and Tracy in Dawn Cave's garden in Melbourne, © 1985 Elisabeth Krause, Sontra

Page **120**: Portrait of Nick Cave, © 1988 Andrew Catlin, London

Page **121**: View from Thomas Wydler's hotel room during the Lollapalooza Festival-Tour in Los Angeles, © 1994 Beate Bartel, Berlin

Page **122 / 123**: Evening mood in Pinheiros, São Paulo. The child in the red T-Shirt on the street is Nick Cave's son, Luke © 1993 Peter Sempel, Hamburg.

Page **126**: Nick Cave and Christoph Dreher at a waterfall in Brazil, © 1993 Beate Bartel, Berlin

Page **133**: Nick Cave during filming of 'Do You Love Me' in Brazil, © 1994 Polly Borland, London

Page **135** (top left): Cave's Manager Rayner Jesson in his Los Angeles hotel room, © 1992 Beate Bartel, Berlin

Page **135** (top right): Matt Crosby asleep in the tour bus during the Lollapalooza Festival-Tour, © 1994 Beate Bartel, Berlin

Page **135** (bottom): Typical backstage room somewhere in the USA during the Lollapalooza Festival-Tour, © 1994 Kai Reinhardt, Dortmund

Page **136**: Nick Cave during filming for 'Do You Love Me' in Brazil, © 1994 Polly Borland, London

Page **137**: View from a window at the Mariott Hotel in Miami, Florida, © 1994 Kai Reinhardt, Dortmund

Page **138**: Nick Cave and Christoph Dreher looking for neighbours somewhere in West London, © 1988 Ellen El Malki, Berlin

Page **139**: Nick Cave and Pedro in Pedro's Bar, Via Madallena in São Paulo (from the film 'Jonas In The Desert' by Peter Sempel), © 1993 Peter Sempel, Hamburg

Page **140**: Nick and Vivian, São Paulo city as backdrop, © 1991 Ellen El Malki, Berlin

Page **141**: Nick and Luke, © 1993 Peter Sempel, Hamburg

Page **142 / 143**: Bad Seeds performance on the 'Conan O' Brian Show' in New York, Summer '94 (left to right: Mick Harvey, Jim Sclavunos, Martyn P. Casey, Thomas Wydler, Nick Cave, Conway Savage, James Johnston), © 1994 Kai Reinhardt, Dortmund

Page **144**: Paul Beares, Nick Cave and some of the musicians from George Clinton's Parliament during the Lollapalooza Festival-Tour in Los Angeles, © 1994 Beate Bartel, Berlin

Page **145**: Portrait of Nick Cave, Los Angeles, © 1992 Anton Corbijn, London

Page **146 / 147**: Set photo of Kylie Minogue during filming of the video for 'Where The Wild Roses Grow', © 1994 David Tonge, London

Page **150**: Portrait of Nick Cave for The Daily Telegraph Saturday Magazine, © 1998 Polly Borland, London

Page **152**: © 1996 Richard Kern, New York / published in Hustler Magazine, August 1996: Volume 23, No. 2, page 10. Reproduction with kind permission of Hustler Magazine.

Page **153**: Celebration to commemorate the award of the first Golden Disc for 'Where The Wild Roses Grow' during the Popkomm fair on 17.8.1996 in Cologne, (left to right standing): Nick Cave, Jim Sclavunos, Blixa Bargeld, Tara-Jane Zagacki (forma Tender Prey), Mick Harvey, Conway Savage; (seated): Martyn P. Casey, Donna Vergier (Mute International), Rayner Jesson (Tender Prey), Tina Funk (forma Mute Deutschland), Thomas Wydler, Jörg Hellwig (forma Intercord), © 1996 Peter Sempel, Hamburg

Page **154**: Nick Cave and Kylie Minogue at The Royal Albert Hall in London, May 20, 1997, © 1997 Joe Dillworth, London

Page **157**: Nick Cave in Hyde Park London. Photo production commissioned by Wire Magazine, © 1999 Frank Bauer, London

Page **158**: Nick Cave on the set of 'Do You Love Me' in São Paulo, © 1994 Polly Borland, London

Page **159**: Portrait of Nick Cave, © 1993 Anton Corbijn, London

Page **160 / 161**: The whole frame of the cover photo, © 1997 Johannes Beck, Berlin

Page **162**: Portrait of Nick Cave with false moustache, © 1988, Anton Corbijn, London. First published in 'Famous Photographs' by Anton Corbijn.

Page **163**: Nick Cave on a bar stool, © 1998 Thomas Rabsch, Cologne

Page **164**: Portrait of Nick Cave, © 1988 Andrew Catlin, London

Page **165**: Nick Cave looking out a window at the Gore Inn, London. Photo production commissioned by Wire Magazine, © 1999 Frank Bauer, London

Page **166 / 167**: Nick Cave listening to music by Samuel Barber in his tidied-up living room in London, © 1997 Thomas Rabsch, Köln

Page **168 / 169**: Nick Cave in Hyde Park London. Photo production commissioned by Wire Magazine, © 1999 Frank Bauer, London

Page **170**: Nick with his first gun at the age of three, © 1960 Dawn Cave, Melbourne. Cave family album. Reproduction with kind permission of Dawn Cave.

Page **174**: The authors: Maximilian Dax and Johannes Beck, © 1999, Oliver Gretscher, minus publishing, Berlin

Back cover (top): Shake hands with Nick Cave! © 1982 Andrew Catlin, London

Back cover (bottom): Portrait of Nick Cave from a photo session for the promotion of 'King Ink', © 1988 Andrew Catlin, London

Beate Bartel

B+T- 003
Postfach 110 680
10836 Berlin. Germany

e-mail: inFo@BeateBartel.de

Frank Bauer

London

Telefon: + 44 - 171 - 375 05 96
Fax: + 44 - 171 - 375 05 96

e-mail: FBauerFB@aol.com

Andrew Catlin

West Hill Lodge
West Hill
Hastings. UK

Phone: + 44 - 836 - 20 94 10
Facsimile: +44 - 1424 - 44 04 24

e-mail: andrewcatlin@usa.net
Internet: www.andrewcatlin.com

Dawn Cave

Dawn Cave is Nicks' mother.

Oliver Gretscher

e-mail: oliver@minus.de

Peter Gruchot

Fotostudio Peter Gruchot
Fürbringer Strasse 7
10996 Berlin. Germany

Tel.+Fax: + 49 - 30 - 691 99 90

Jutta Henglein

Langendreesch 16
14532 Kleinmachnow. Germany

Phone: + 49 - 332 03 - 214 96

Elisabeth Krause

Bahnhofstrasse 3
36205 Sontra. Germany

Phone: + 49 - 5653 - 286

Ellen El Malki

e-mail: ElElectra@aol.com

Stefan Malzkorn

S. Malzkorn / Fotografie / Hamburg

Telefon: + 49 - 40 - 34 54 02

e-mail: malzkornpic@on-line.de

Peter Milne

M · 33 Photoagency
16 Carlisle Avenue
Balaclava Victoria 3183
Australia

Phone: + 61 - 3 - 952 715 47
Facsimile: + 61 - 3 - 952 715 47

Contact: Helen Frayman - M · 33
Photoagency

Thomas Rabsch

Bilderberg
An der Ölmühle 44
51069 Köln. Germany

Phone: + 49 - 221 - 68 48 98
Fax: + 49 - 221 - 68 48 98

e-mail: trabisch@aol.com
Internet: www.bilderberg.com

Kai Reinhardt

(Production manager and sound
engineer of Nick Cave & The Bad
Seeds)

e-mail: monomama@noisyologic.de

Uli M. Schüppel

Schüppel-Produktion/de.flex-film
Husemannstraße 33
10435 Berlin. Germany

Phone: + 49 - 30 - 442 94 57

Internet: www.de.flex-film/com

Nicholas Seferi

12, Alenby Road,
Canterbury 3126
Melbourne. Australia

Peter Sempel

Black Sun Flower Film+Foto
Blitze im Eierbecher
Ohlendorffstraße 18
20535 Hamburg. Germany

Phone: + 49 - 40 - 250 04 68
Fasimile: + 49 - 40 - 319 31 97

Internet: www.sempel.com

Andrew & Lynne Trute

Cave Archives of Australia
Andrew & Lynne Trute
Cave Archives Melbourne

e-mail: andrew.trute@nre.vic.gov.au

Ross Waterman

388 A High Street
Prahran Victoria 3181
Australia

Phone: + 61 - 3 - 951 057 63
Facsimile: + 61 - 3 - 930 700 78
Mobile: + 61 - 412 - 68 67 43

e-mail: dedes@excite.com ‑

The Photographers

Rainer Berson

Liechtensteinstrasse 42/6a
1090 Wien. Austria

Phone: + 43 - 1 - 317 12 77

e-mail: rainer.berson@teleweb.at

Polly Borland

Light Industry
Simon Crocker
51-53 Mount Pleasant
London WC1X OAE. UK

Phone: + 44 - 171 - 831 30 33
Facsimile: + 44 - 171 - 405 37 21
Mobile: + 44 - 410 - 513 098

e-mail: swcrocker@btconnect.com

Jeff Busby

Busby Photography
148 A Barkley Street
St. Kilda 3182
Australia

Phone: + 61 -3 - 95 25 35 85
Facsimile: + 61 - 3 - 95 25 35 85

e-mail: jefbusby@ozemail.com.av
Internet: www.jeffbusby.com

Anton Corbijn

e-mail: corbijn@corbijn.co.uk

Joe Dilworth

174 Camden Road
London NW1 9HJ. UK

Phone: + 44 - 171 - 485 19 09

Anno Dittmer

Brunhildstrasse 8a
10829 Berlin. Germany

Phone: + 49 - 30 - 781 27 56
Facsimile: + 49 - 30 - 781 27 56

e-mail: anno.dittmer@berlin.de

English / Goldman

Evan English
Outlaw Values
50 Bonnington Square
London SW8 1TQ. UK

Paul Goldman
King Mob Pictures P/L
Sydney. Australia

Petra Gall

Potsdamer Strasse 155
10783 Berlin. Germany

Phone: + 49 - 30 - 216 43 13
Facsimile: + 49 - 30 - 216 43 13

Every effort has been made to trace the copyright holders of the photographs in this book but one or two were unreachable. We would be grateful if the photographers concerned would contact us.

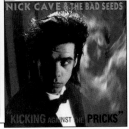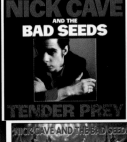

Discography

THE BOYS NEXT DOOR

Albums and miscellaneous releases

1978 'Lethal Weapons' (LP), containing 3 Boys Next Door tracks
1979 'Door Door' (LP/CD)
+   'Scatterbrain'
1979 'Hee Haw' (EP)
1980 'The Boys Next Door', identical to the LP 'The Birthday Party'

THE BIRTHDAY PARTY

Album releases, CDBonus-Tracks, and Single B-Sides

1980 'The Birthday Party', identical to the LP 'The Boys Next Door'
1981 'Prayers On Fire' (LP/CD)
+   'Blundertown'
+   'Cathy's Kisses'
1982 'Junkyard' (LP/CD)
+   'Release The Bats'
+   'Blast Off'
+   'Dead Joe' (Version)
1982 'Drunk On The Pope's Blood' (Live-EP incl. songs by
       Lydia Lunch / Live-CD incl. 4 songs from the 'A Collection'-EP)
1983 'The Bad Seed' (EP)
1983 'Mutiny' (EP)
1989 'Mutiny/The Bad Seed' (CD)
+   'Pleasure Avalanche'
+   'The Six Strings That Drew Blood'
1985 'A Collection' (EP of rarities,
       included on CD 'Drunk On The Pope's Blood')
1985 'It's Still Living' (LP/CD), Live
1987 'The Peel Sessions: The Birthday Party' (EP/CD)
1988 'The Peel Sessions: The Birthday Party II' (EP/CD)
1988 'Hee-Haw' (CD), including the LP 'The Birthday Party'
1992 'Hits' (CD), Compilation
1993 'The Fullness Of His Coming'
       (Song on the Anita-Lane-CD 'Dirty Pearl')
1999 'Live 1981-82' (CD), Live

DIE HAUT

Album releases with the participation of Nick Cave

1983 'Der karibische Western' (12'), Cave whistles on 1 track
1983 'Burning The Ice' (LP), Cave sings 4 songs
1988 'Headless Body In Topless Bar' (LP/CD) Cave sings 1 song
1993 'Sweat' (LP/CD), Live, Cave sings 3 songs
1993 'Sweat' (Video), Live, Cave sings 4 songs

NICK CAVE AND THE BAD SEEDS

Album releases, CDBonus-Tracks and Single B-Sides

1984 'From Her To Eternity' (LP/CD)
+   'In The Ghetto'
+   'The Moon Is In The Gutter'
+   'From Her To Eternity',
       (Version off the soundtrack 'Wings of Desire')
1984 'The Firstborn Is Dead' (LP/CD)
+   'The Six Strings That Drew Blood'
+   'Tupelo' (Single Edit)
1986 'Kicking Against The Pricks' (LP/CD)
+   'Running Scared'
+   'Black Betty'
1986 'Your Funeral, My Trial' (2x12'/CD)
+   'Scum'
1988 'Tender Prey' (LP/CD)
+   'The Mercy Seat' (Video Edit)
+   'Girl At The Bottom Of My Glass'
1989 'Ghosts ... Of The Civil Dead' (LP/CD), Soundtrack
1990 'The Good Son' (LP/CD)
+   'The Weeping Song' (Remix)
+   'The Train Song'
+   'Helpless'
+   'Cocks'n'Asses' = 'The B-Side Song'
+   'Acoustic Versions From Tender Prey', 3 songs
1992 'Henry's Dream' (LP/CD)
+   'Blue Bird'
+   'What Can I Give You?' (France)
+   'Jack The Ripper' (Acoustic Version)
+   'The Mercy Seat' (Live)
+   'The Carny' (Live)
+   'The Ship Song' (Live)
+   'I Had A Dream, Joe' (Live)
+   'The Good Son' (Live)
1992   **'What A Wonderful World'** (CDM),
       Duet with Shane McGowan
1993 'Live Seeds' (CD)
1994 'Let Love In' (LP/CD)
+   'Sail Away'
+   'Do You Love Me?' (Single Edit)
+   'Loverman' (Single Edit)
+   'B-Side'
+   '(I'll Love You) Till The End Of The World'
+   'That's What Jazz Is To Me'
+   'Where The Action Is'
1996 'Murder Ballads' (LP/CD)
+   'The Ballad Of Robert Moore And Betty Coltrane'
+   'The Willow Garden'
+   'King Kong Kitchee Kitchee Ki-Mi-O'
+   'Knoxville Girl'
1996 'To Have And To Hold' (CD), Soundtrack
1997 'The Boatman's Call' (LP/CD)
+   'Little Empty Boat'
+   'Right Now I'm A-Roaming'
+   'Come Into My Sleep'
+   'Black Hair' (Band Version)
+   'Babe I Got You Bad'
1998   **'Live At The Royal Albert Hall'** (CD)
1998 'The Best Of' (LP/CD), Compilation
1999 'And The Ass Saw The Angel' (LP/CD), Readings

OTHER NICK CAVE RELEASES

1985   **'Vixo'**   'Kickabye' by Annie Hogan (LP)
1989   **'Helpless'** on 'The Bridge: A Tribute to Neil Young' (LP/CD)
1991   **'Tower Of Song'** on
         I'm Your Fan – The Songs Of Leonard Cohen'   (LP/CD)
1993   **'Faraway, So Close'** and **'Cassiel's Song'** on
         'Faraway, So Close' (Soundtrack)
1995   **'There Is a Light'** on 'Batman Forever' (Soundtrack-CD)
1995   2 duets on 'The World's A Girl' by Anita Lane (CDM)
1996   2 hidden tracks with The Dirty Three on
         'X-Files: Songs In The Key Of X' (Soundtrack-CD)
1996   **'The Sweetest Embrace'** on
         'Oedipus Schmoedipus' by Barry Adamson (CD)
1997   **'Mack The Knife'** on 'Kurt Weill: September Songs' (CD)
1997   **'The Big Hurt'** and   **'Mojo-Soho'** on 'Mojo' (Soundtrack)

FILMS

1984   **'The City'** by Heiner Mühlenbrock
1988   **'Dandy'** by Peter Sempel
1988   **'Wings of Desire'** by Wim Wenders
1989   **'Ghosts ... Of The Civil Dead'** by John Hillcoat
1991   **'Just Visiting This Planet'** by Peter Sempel
1991   **'Johnny Suede'** by Tom DiCillo
1991   **'Until The End Of The World'** by Wim Wenders
1994   **'Jonas (Mekas) In The Desert'** by Peter Sempel
1996   **'Rhinoceros Hunting In Budapest'** by Michael Hausman
2000   **'Jonas (Mekas) At The Ocean'** by Peter Sempel

VIDEOS

1982   **'The Last Birthday Party'** by Heiner Mühlenbrock,
         documentary
1987   **'Kings Of Independence'**,   2 songs by Cave/Bad Seeds
1988   **'Pleasure Heads Must Burn'**, Birthday Party Live
1991   **'The Road To God Knows Where'** by Uli Schüppel,
         Documentary
1992   **'Live At The Paradiso'** by John Hillcoat
1998   **'The Videos'**, Video compilation
1998   **'The Garden's Voice'**, Cave sings 3 songs solo
1998   **'Lending The Garden a Voice'**, Cave sings 2 further songs

BOOKS

1988   **'King Ink'**, Song texts and prose
1988   **'And the Ass saw the Angel'**, Novel
1993   **'AS-FIX-E-8'**, Comic by Lydia Lunch and Nick Cave
1993   **'Fish In A Barrel'** by Peter Milne, preface by Nick Cave
1998   **'King Ink II'**, Song texts and prose
1998   **'The Gospel According To Mark'**, introduction by Nick Cave

       Plus **various articles** in UK daily papers.

Internet-Links:
http://www.mutelibtech.com (official contact)

Art direction and picture editor: Johannes Beck
Cover photo: Johannes Beck
Cover artwork: Max Bauer
Typography: Max Bauer
Scans and image treatment: Oliver Gretscher / minus Verlag

Text: Maximilian Dax
Editor original text: Johannes Beck
Translations: Ian Minnock
Editor English translation: Maximilian Dax
Final editors: Maria Zinfert, Karla Handwerker, Antje Block
Quotes: Violetta Cyrol, Nicole Himmerlein / die zuständige agentur Berlin

Revision: Beck+Bauer
Preprint: die gestalten verlag

Commissioned by Robert Klanten / die gestalten verlag Berlin

www.minus.de

The Authors

Johannes Beck, born 1959 in Wetzlar, Germany, is the owner of the renowned graphic agency minus Verlag in Berlin. After finishing school he worked as a designer for the Frankfurt-based magazine Pflasterstrand (editor: Daniel Cohn-Bendit), before he moved to Berlin in 1981 to become a freelance art director for amnesty international, Mute Records, the Bundesbildungswerk et al as well as an illustrator for the German daily newspaper Frankfurter Rundschau. Corporate Designs incl. the international jazz school in Palermo, Nick Cave and the Bad Seeds („Murder Ballads", „Boatman's Call", „Best Of"), Einstürzende Neubauten, Bob Rutman, the annual „Warten", the play „Sid & Nancy" by Ben Becker and many others.

Maximilian Dax, born in 1969 in Kiel, Germany, grew up in Germany and Italy, works as freelance journalist, artists consultant and graphic artist in Berlin and Hamburg. From 1990 until 1992 PA to The Gun Club, publisher and chief editor of the magazines Alert and Sonic Press. Corporate designs incl. Pole, Gaz Varley (LFO), Nick Holder. Together with Francesco Sbano and Peter Cadera publisher of the CD-Compilation „Il canto di malavita – The Music of the Mafia" (will be published in Spring 2000).
Interviews, features, columns and reports et al for Die Tageszeitung, Tempo, Der Spiegel, Freak.

The authors would like to thank Nick Cave, Anita Lane, Mick Harvey, Dawn Cave, Sarah Lowe (Mute Press Department), Julie Sersansie und Rayner Jesson (Tender Prey Management), Anne Berning (Mute Germany), Ian Minnock, Antje Block, Karla Handwerker, Beate Bartel, Thomas Wydler, Christoph Dreher, Ellen El Malki, Maria Zinfert, Nick Seferi, Mariella Del Conte, Alexander Hacke, Jochen Arbeit, Lynne und Andrew Trute, Remo Park, Oliver Gretscher, Violetta Cyrol, Nicole Himmerlein, Ralf Struntz, Elisabeth Krause, James Baes, Robert Klanten, Hendrik Hellige, Tina Funk, Heiner Mühlenbrock, Angelika Staiger, Arto Lindsay, Andrew Catlin, Kai Reinhardt, Jessamy Calkin, Helen Freyman, John Hillcoat, Daniel Miller, Erik Hess, Andreas Banaski, Diamanda Galas, Henry Rollins, Lydia Lunch, Sybille Schön, David Tonge, Peter Milne, u.d. Bauer, Tom DiCillo, Ross Waterman, Uli M. Schüppel, Jeff Busby, Blixa Bargeld, Frank Behnke, Frank Bauer, Anton Corbijn, Thomas Rabsch, Rainer Berson, Polly Borland, Petra Gall, Anno Dittmer, Henrike Eicke, Donald Völker, Jutta Henglein, Caspar Brötzmann, Sibylle Trenck, Stefan Malzkorn, Peter Gruchot, Peter Cadera, Joe Dilworth, Lisa Bauer, RA Dr. Moog, Stefan Strüver, Tristan Thönnissen, Michael Sheehy, www.iae.nl/users/maes/cave/#news and especially Bleddyn Butcher (for stealing our time) and Dietke Steck and Simone Rau for their angel-like patience and for just being wonderful!

Die Deutsche Bibliothek-
CIP Einheitsaufnahme

Dax, Maximilian:
The Life and Music of Nick Cave: an illustrated biography/
Design: Johannes Beck, Text: Maximilian Dax-
Berlin: Die- Gestalten- Ver., dgv, 1999
Deutsche Ausgabe ISBN 3- 931126-29-3
English Version ISBN 3- 931126-27-7

The Life and Music of Nick Cave

printed by Medialis Offset, Berlin
Made in Europe

dgv- Die Gestalten Verlag, Berlin
Fax: +49. 30. 30871068
Email: verlag@die-gestalten.de
www.die-gestalten.de

Distributed/ represented through:

USA / Canada:

Consortium BSD
1045 Westgate Drive
St. Paul
Minnesota 55114/ 1065
Fon: +1. 651. 221 90 35
Fax: +1. 651. 917 64 06
Email: mail@cbsd.com

Great Britain / Ireland / Asia/ Scandinavia:

Art Books International
1 Stewart´s Court 220 Steward´s Rd
London SW 8 4UD
Fon: +44. 171. 720 15 03
Fax: +44. 171. 720 31 58
Email: mail@art-bks.com

Japan:

Infinite Books
1-25-2 Nishihara, Shibuya-ku
Tokyo
Fon: +81. 3. 346 95708
Fax: +81. 3. 346 95708

Deutschland:

LKG
Pötzschauer Weg
D - 04579 Espenhain
Tel: +49 34206 65121
Fax: +49 34206 65110

In case you should have problems finding
our books in your country, please contact
dgv directly or look up our website.

BLAG
edited by Sally and Sarah Edwards
160 pages, 24,4 x 30,5 cm
full colour, approx. 200 photos, Softcover
DM 69 £ 24.99 $ 39.99 ••• ISBN 3-931126-31-5

SPARK
by Dirk Rudolph
160 pages, 24 x 28 cm
full colour, approx. 200 illustrations, Softcover
DM 69 £ 24.99 $ 39.99 ••• 3-931126-33-1

POP TICS
by Bungalow Records
edited by H. Beier, M. Liesenfeld / Bungalow
40 pages, 15 x 15 cm,
special see-through box, including free audio CD
DM 29.90 £ 12.99 $ 19.99 ••• ISBN 3-931126-30-7
release: November '99

RADICAL EYE
by Miron Zownir
160 pages, 24 x 30 cm
duotone, approx. 150 photos, German/English
DM 49,90 $ 27,99 £ 18,99 ••• ISBN 3-931126-13-7

HÖR MIT SCHMERZEN - LISTEN WITH PAIN
edited by Klaus Maeck
132 pages, 23 x 30 cm
approx. 170 b/w photos, Softcover
DM 35 $ 25 £ 13,99 ••• ISBN 3-931126-09-9

REDEMPTION
by Floria Sigismondi
160 pages, 24 x 33 cm
full colour, approx. 200 photos, Hardcover
DM 89 £ 29.90 $ 50 ••• ISBN 3-931126-18-8

LOCALIZER 1.3 - ICONS
edited by B. Richard, R. Klanten, S. Heidenreich
176 pages, 24 x 30 cm
full colour, special 3D Softcover, English Version
176 Seiten, 24 x 30 cm
vollfarbig, 3D-Sondereinband, Deutsche Version
DM 69 £ 24.99 $ 44 ••• ISBN 3-931126-04-8

LOCALIZER 1.2 - SURREALITY
edited by Robert Klanten, Andreas Peyerl
192 pages, 24 x 30 cm,
full colour, approx. 220 photos, special 3D Softcover
DM 69 £ 24.99 $ 44 ••• ISBN 3-931126-03-X

LODOWN - GRAPHIC ENGINEERING
by Marok
Thomas Marecki a.k.a. Marok
176 pages, 29 x 22 cm,
landscape format, full colour, Softcover
DM 59 £ 24.99 $ 39.99 ••• ISBN 3-931126-16-1